STOCK MANTHAN

The Hunt for **Multi-Bagger Stocks**

Unveiling a World of
Relaxed Value Investing for Superlative Returns

I0490532

CA NITIN SHARMA

INDIA · SINGAPORE · MALAYSIA

Notion Press

No.8, 3rd Cross Street,
CIT Colony, Mylapore,
Chennai, Tamil Nadu – 600004

First Published by Notion Press 2020
Copyright © CA Nitin Sharma 2020
All Rights Reserved.

ISBN

Paperback: 978-1-64951-973-3
Hardcase: 978-1-64951-997-9

Lost money and said bye-bye to stock market—the story seems true, but it doesn't feel good.

Gained money and created wealth from stock market—the story doesn't seem true, but it feels good.

Let's make the second feel-good story one of the most beautiful truths of life.

– CA Nitin Sharma

CONTENTS

SECTION - 3: POST ACQUISITION ANALYSIS AND SALE

SECTION - 4: DON'T FOLLOW THE LOSER'S PATH AND DO WHAT WINNERS DO

SECTION - 5: SUM UP OF STOCK MANTHAN PROCESS THROUGH ILLUSTRATIONS

ACKNOWLEDGEMENT

Since the beginning of 2020, I had plans to prepare and release this book to share the strategies, processes and concepts which helps me in my investment journey.

I would like to thank my parents for supporting me through every walk of life and also to my wife, sister and brother-in-law for supporting and appreciating the idea of bringing this book to readers. They were also the primary audience for the manuscript and gave honest reviews about each portion of the book.

Apart from this, I am also thankful to:

- All my friends-cum-students who admired my efforts to develop strategies, as this worked for their portfolio too in addition to mine

- Microsoft for their efficient tools, especially MS Excel, which is not only important for managing my day-to-day professional tasks but also for creating and maintaining the necessary database to support my investment decisions and also for MS Word which helped prepare this manuscript

- Last but not the least, the team at Notion Press for being my self-publishing guide and for their serious efforts regarding the beautification of this book and ensuring its reach through various channels.

ABOUT THE BOOK

There are two facts pertinent to the stock market:

1. All the information can be made easily available, which is required to analyze and find the stocks that have the ability to provide multi-bagger returns in the future

2. Around 80-85% of people lose money in the stock market

The irony is that both the above-mentioned statements are equally true. They are true even when the first one depicts that stock markets are not risky at all, but the second one tells that the stock market is a place where one can get his hands burnt easily.

This sarcastic situation arises because a majority of people do not understand the power of the first fact, which is easily available analytical data. They just try to shoot their arrow in the dark. They try to speed up their vehicle without learning how to drive fast or without even learning how to drive. At last, they end up proving the second fact i.e. a majority of investors become losers. The panacea for this problem is only one—learning by oneself—"How to invest in a consistently profitable manner?"

For this, an investor has to strive to find answers to the following questions:

1. How to identify stocks which have the potential to give multi-bagger returns?

2. What steps are necessary to maintain a portfolio of stocks in a manner that generates consistent returns and avoids losses?

3. How to develop a mindset which helps avoid the mistakes generally made by people who lose in the market?

It is my honest attempt to help readers find answers to the above questions in this book. This book includes all possible aspects to find out multi-bagger stocks, which means stocks whose prices may double or more in the near future (the next one or two years).

Apart from this, the analysis done by the author in the past to judge multi-bagger potential in various stocks is included as illustrations to provide a clear idea on how to evaluate the various parameters of a stock before deciding to invest in it in the long run.

THE DILEMMA OF AN INVESTOR AND THE WAY TO COME OUT

Hi,

In terms of your personal experience in the stock market and the fact that you chose to read this book, you may be

- A newbie who is quite ambitious with a goal to make it big in the market but don't know how

- A trader or investor without good experience in the stock market who wants to regain the amount lost in the market and earn surplus by learning the principles of "How to find and invest in multi-bagger stocks?"

- A trader or investor with good experience in the market who wants to take an initiative to learn the stock market principles to earn in an even better style

This book aims at fulfilling all your expectations. But whoever you are in the above category, you need to have one thing clear in your mind before proceeding—you will never get what you desire until you deserve the same. In short, Deserve your Desire.

How do you deserve your desire in case of the stock market?

The answer lies in believing only one truth forever,

> "Fabulous earnings in the stock market don't require hard work but a continuous series of smart work.
>
> Money will work for you in achieving this objective, but managing it to do the same will be your responsibility and nobody else's."

It should be clear to everyone that buying a stock isn't like buying a piece of paper or some investment units held in electronic form; in fact, this means you are buying a small portion of a particular company. Hence, the analysis which is required to take a decision as to whether or not you should own or partially own a running business couldn't be significantly different from what caution is required to buy a company's shares. In other words, the attitude of selecting stocks like selecting vegetables or grocery items in a store should be immediately stopped, and a prudent mindset is to be developed, which allows the investor to select the right stocks in a way one has to choose the right business to purchase.

How to work smartly and when? This book tends to develop related attributes in readers' minds which can benefit them for a lifetime. There is a thorough attempt to keep the content limited to what is important for you as an investor, which means sufficient, concrete and practical descriptions of do's and don'ts, investment in equity versus anything else, the real meaning of equity and the exact process, including formulae, to identify potential stocks at the right time which means at the right price. Furthermore, the process of finding multi-bagger stocks is followed by personal experiences, observations and illustrations involving actual decision-making procedures in the past.

Believe me, the content was drafted while assuming myself in the place of a reader as:

- A novice investor who urges to make it in the market, surviving the wave and avoiding any possible disaster

- An experienced investor who had a very sad tenure in the market and is in search of a tool that can prove to be a turning point in his journey

Also, the language used is such that one can experience a teacher sitting nearby and stating the principles to be applied one by one and the ambiguity to be avoided in terms of value investing in the stock market. I relived my experience of learning the techniques years ago and designed all the content in the way I wished to learn before getting into the market 10 years ago and also at the time I failed in the beginning with the wrong approach and was in the process of re-engineering my strategies.

Throughout my journey in the stock market, I also realized that more than the formulae and concepts I learned and the procedures I developed, what helped me was the desire to change my mindset to adopt strategies in the required manner, which means developing myself spiritually for achieving what I desired. Surprisingly, whatever one achieves in one's lifespan is 20% due to the knowledge and techniques embedded in his mind while the remaining 80% is due to his wilful attitude and mindset. This is the sound reason why a college drop-out managed to become the world's richest man, and how the poor guy, who once served as a petrol pump attendant, managed to build a business and crown his family the richest one in India in current terms.

Investing in stocks is not an exception. Hence, apart from describing the practical steps to be undertaken by an investor to make it big in the stock market, this book also emphasizes, in a brief manner, the necessary spiritual state to be held by an investor. There is no alternative to adopting the right approach in the field of stocks, but beyond that, it is a bigger truth that success in this field will come to an investor only with the attainment of the required spiritual development i.e. an attitude or mindset free from greed, fear, unrest, distrust, procrastination or any such disturbing factors. Many a time, it's a difficult task to develop the same mindset in most people with respect to every walk of life, but surprisingly, such spirituality can be achieved in the limited context of successful investing in the stock market through dedicated and committed learning of:

1. What to do? This includes
   - Properly selecting a value stock
   - Identifying the correct time to purchase

- Remaining invested for the required period

- Disposal at the correct time

2. What not to do? This includes

  - Selection of stock without self-analyzing

  - Not allocating the correct proportion of the portfolio to a particular stock

  - Holding a stock for lesser or more period than what is actually permitted by that stock's fundamental indications

  - Involving unnecessary emotions in managing a portfolio

Saying that the stock market is risky won't be enough without adding that the risk comes with the uncertainty of outcome and uncertainty of outcome results when the actions chosen are not in proper connection with the desired outcome. If one opts to choose methods bound to result in loss of money, then he cannot escape responsibility saying that the stock market is risky and he bears no mistake. He commits the mistake of not being in the market but of choosing stocks without self-analysis.

If you have suffered a loss in the share market until now, it is not a big deal. Many retail investors face the same. What matters is what you opt after that. This makes the difference among 80% gainers and 20% losers in the stock market. Instead of taking it as your fate, if you determine to train your mind perfectly to opt only value stocks hereafter instead of blindly investing in any stock, things will change gradually. There may even come a point in your life when you begin to earn a major proportion of your income from merely investing in equity. The only thing to remember is that you should not stop dreaming, and the dream has to be big enough. The seed of dream turns into the tree of reality only when it is equipped with belief, dedication, determination and discipline. Scrap your past to welcome the beautiful future waiting ahead.

You are supposed to refer to anything else in addition to this for further motivation because from my perspective, the desire for financial freedom and wealth creation are the main ingredients for anyone to develop as a value investor, and if you chose to read the book on this subject, you more or less desire both of these, isn't it? This is why strict focus is on what to do and what not. Then the only thing you require is an attitude, which helps you desire financial freedom and wealth creation, plus the perfect approach for taking decisions to invest in stock(s) along with a strong determination to achieve the same, come what may.

Don't think it's the prerogative of only CA/finance/commerce background people to read financial statements in relation to successful investing. Any person from whatsoever background or score during school or college can carry out the analyses required to invest. Warren Buffet started reading companies' balance sheets barely at the age of 12. During his school life, he chose to make extra money to invest in stocks by selling newspapers, golf balls and stamps and detailing cars among other means. Today, he is the third richest person in the world on the basis of his investing experience.

What's the excuse in your mind? Leave every excuse and start.

Happy learning and earning!

Regards,

CA Nitin Sharma

SECTION - 1

WEALTH CREATION
AND EQUITY

CHAPTER 1

WEALTH CREATION – VICTORY OF INCOME OVER INFLATION

[1]

"Wealth creation is a snake and ladder game, which every individual needs to play by default in his life, be it a salaried person, self-employed person, businessman or entrepreneur."

---

[1]

In the above writing, 'ladder' refers to earnings which are essential for fulfilling the present and future needs in the form of savings, and 'snake' refers to inflation in the economy, which diminishes the purchasing power of money held by a person with the passage of time. The number of snakes will always be constant, but we can work on increasing the number and size of ladders so that we reach from zero to hundred quickly."

In a nation like India, where the average inflation rate falls between 8-10% and the rate of interest on fixed deposits range from 6-7%, there is no need to say that if we invest our savings in fixed deposits, the returns will not be able to meet the inflation rate and the value of our savings will decline over a period of time.

One can spend Rs 100 today to buy an article worth Rs 100. But if he chooses to keep Rs 100 invested in fixed deposit for the next year, then it will become Rs 107 along with interest earned upon that. But even with that Rs 107 in hand, he won't be able to buy that article which was within his budget one year ago. This is because after considering the average inflation rate, the price of that article will become Rs 108-110 after one year. Furthermore, the income of Rs 7 earned by investing Rs 100 will be subject to tax at a rate ranging from 5% to 30%, which will further deteriorate the amount left in hand on a net basis. It can be clearly observed in this example that the value of money has declined in terms of its purchasing power.

This scenario will definitely arrive if one opts to keep Rs 100 in fixed deposit to get Rs 107 after one year and was not at all curious to find a source through which he can turn that Rs 100 into Rs 120. If he chooses to invest in an alternative which can provide a return of Rs 20 over Rs 100 invested in a year, then he can not only buy that article for Rs 110, but he can save Rs 10 in hand after purchasing that article. This is real savings.

No wonder people do not feel like having ample money in their hands during retirement. This is because

- They do not invest in the option which provides optimum returns

- They invest in the wrong option
- They invest in the right option but in the wrong way

For need of any further example, you can search on Google. Let's head towards some important discussion now.

[2]

"Being conservative and avoiding risk is not always favourable; sometimes avoiding manageable risk is even riskier.

When it comes to wealth creation, which is the dream of almost every individual, measured risks are worth taking. Risks have to be managed in such a manner that it seems RISKLESS."

---

[2]

An investment option which can give superlative returns will bear some sort of risk. But when it comes to life, its alternate name is 'risk'. I ride a bike; there is a risk of an accident. I walk under a bridge; the bridge may fall upon me. I go by flight; it may crash. There are multiple things that can happen to me, which can even eliminate me from this planet. But thinking about all this, I cannot stop riding a bike because the risk of an accident is very minimal in comparison to its need as a conveyance or for the fun of riding it if I am a biker. I cannot stop walking under a bridge if that is the only way to reach my destination or if that is the shortest way of doing so. I cannot avoid going by flight due to the risk of crashing as the need to reach my destination faster is worthier and probable.

In the same way, the need for financial freedom is much more important than the risk involved in achieving the same through potential investment options, which are better than riskless investment options like fixed deposits.

Keep in mind that the risk mentioned is not of a kind where one jumps into an unknown river without knowing swimming and cries for help. Not only does he need to learn swimming, but he should also develop a habit of testing the depth of the river by sinking only one foot first. In this way, the RISK can be converted into MEASURED RISK. The need to learn swimming actually signifies learning "How to find value stocks to invest in the equity market?" and testing the depth means "How to proceed carefully in the beginning and how to manage the situation thereafter?"

The only question which arises while investing in such options is "How can the risk involved be minimized such that it maintains the overall returns on the portfolio in the positive side?" This is the only thing to be worked out, and my purpose is to lead you in that direction.

[3]

"Equity and real estate are the two investment options which can provide above-inflation returns. But equity stands far better."

---

[3]

People invest in real estate i.e. land/flat/building with a hope or belief to get a rise in price with the passage of time and thus increase the value of the amount invested. It ought to be a good investment vehicle, but it is not as good as investment in equity in present times due to the following reasons:

- Initial investment in the stock market can be as low as Rs 10,000 or even lower. However, investing in real estate surely involves a huge amount, which makes it not within the reach of every investor

- Investment just in a few clicks over a desktop, laptop or even mobile is possible in the case of equity but not in the case of real estate

- Acquiring and selling equity investment is quite viable. You can purchase and sell anytime. But this is not the case for real estate

- Price transparency and accessibility is quite high in equity as the equity market is highly regulated while the same is not the case for real estate. It's not easy to calculate the fair value to know whether the quotation is favourable or not

Apart from all this, finding multi-bagger stocks after legitimate analysis and investing in them at the correct time for an adequate duration before sale off generally provides higher returns than that possible with real estate investments. I am telling this from my personal experience.

CHAPTER 2

EQUITY – FACTS AND MYTHS

[4]

"Equity market investments are not risky at all. But people opt riskier ways to meet their goal for wealth maximization through stocks, and this results in wealth deterioration rather than creation.

Either by investing directly in stocks or listing their companies in the stock market, almost every billionaire has been able to create enormous wealth. Then how can the stock market be risky? The path opted by retail investors is often risky and not the market."

[4]

80-85% of investors lose money in the stock market. This is quite shocking and the reason behind this is only one—they couldn't differentiate between investing and gambling. They claim they have made investments in equity, but the fact is that people generally try their luck by putting their money in one or more stocks without any proper reason. They invest either by referring to some free tips or on the advice of their friends or from any other such baseless sources. The only medicine to cure this kind of mentality is to learn the method to identify stocks which have a strong tendency to grow consistently over a period of time.

The first thing to be kept in mind in order to learn "How to identify multi-bagger stocks?" is—the movement of the price of a stock eventually depends upon the growth prospects of the company's underlying business and its management. Hence, before investing in any stock, it is imperative to know about the growth prospects of the company in the near future after studying its business with the help of available tools. Without undergoing this step, the risk can never be eliminated, and the responsibility of facing negative outcomes will be of the investor and not the market.

Had the stock market been a risky investment alternative, Warren Buffet would not have been the third richest person in the world just by investing in stocks, and this couldn't have proved true for ace Indian investor, Rakesh Jhunjhunwala as well. The only thing they did was they converted the risks associated with the stock market into measured risks. Then why do 80% of investors lose their money in the stock market? Because they do not recognize this concept.

They succeed just because they have one thing in common—choosing quality stocks with multi-bagger potential and holding the investment for a considerably long period with strict principles for a timely exit.

You should also not focus on short-term methods; rather concentrate on imitating the actions of these billionaire investors in the correct way. The obvious questions which may arise are:

1. What are multi-bagger stocks?

2. How to identify multi-bagger stocks?

3. What are the principles governing the buying and selling of a stock?

4. How to monitor the portfolio regularly?

This book is a serious attempt to answer all these questions.

[5]

"Stock analysis and investing is not rocket science, but it needs a little conscience.

Develop that conscience with respect to the stock market. Just assume that you do not know anything about it. This is the first step towards having wisdom in any field. So the same also holds true in investing."

---

[5]

To use a mobile or computer, you don't need to learn the mechanism of the machine; you just need to know how to use the different functions and software installed in it. Applying the same logic to investing, there is no need to get into unnecessary jargon by trying to understand the things which are not at all necessary to become a great value investor. Whether you are

- A novice investor

- A losing investor

- A gaining but more ambitious investor

It will be helpful if you assume you are not aware of anything on "How to hunt for multi-bagger stocks?" before going ahead in the journey of obtaining the concepts mentioned in this book. This is because an empty glass is easy to fill with milk, but if the glass is already filled with water, there is no place to put milk in it. Just scrap all the half-natured prenotions before going ahead, and you will save a lot of time and energy.

[6]

"There is enough on this earth for everyone's need but not for everyone's greed. In the same way, the market has the potential to provide superlative returns, which will increase with more and more experience while following the right path. But expectations like building 'Rome in one day' are not possible on any planet."

---

[6]

With more and more experience, the earnings one gets from his portfolio will improve as he masters the principles and obtains wisdom gradually. But notions like expecting returns of 50% in a month or getting the total amount invested in all the stocks doubled in 3-6 months will not work in the real world.

The fact must be accepted that if your portfolio is able to fetch returns at around three times the returns provided by banks on fixed deposits, then it is fair enough. As we know, the return on fixed deposits stands at 6-7% as of now. So if you manage your portfolio and get returns ranging from 20-25% annually on a compounding basis, you are good to go. Beyond that is all bonus and most welcome. It doesn't mean you should not strive to maintain the portfolio to earn as much as possible and even beyond 25%, but you need to be satisfied with annualized returns at the rate of 25% if you are maintaining a portfolio with adequate proportion of real multi-bagger shares. It's enough, and there would be no surprise in telling that the wealthiest investor in the world i.e. Warren Buffet created his fortune with compounding growth over his portfolio at a similar rate i.e. around 25% over the last 60 years. Compounding growth means we earn 25% on 1 lakh invested in the portfolio, and the next year, we have around 25% again on 1.25 lakhs. In this way, wealth will be created. Meanwhile, fresh investments are to be added, and automatically, the value of all the investments together may rise so much that one could meet all his requirements.

[7]

"Stock market—the field with the greatest number of self-claimed experts, who are not able to change their fortune with their investments but claim to change yours. Take the sword in your own hands and fight your battle instead of believing them to do it for you."

---

[7]

The stock market is one of the rare fields where people who travel by public transport teach moneymaking methods to people who travel by car, and surprisingly, the car owners are convinced too. My intent here is different and is not meant to hurt anybody.

If a person knows about a mine where diamonds lie underneath, and he offers to hand over the map to reach the mine by demanding some silver coins in return, does it make any practical sense? Yes, it may be possible that such a person tells me the location of the mine so that I also benefit by digging diamonds, but that will only come out of his generosity and not by seeking some silver coins as consideration. Now compare this situation with a person, who is a self-claimed expert, offering some stock tips which are sure to give twice or thrice the returns for their nominal fees. Both are the same stand. Had they been clear about the tactics to make it in the market in a profitable way in the long run, they would have been doing it for themselves instead of contacting us to make us believe they can manage our money better than us. No wonder around 85% of people generally suffer loss in the market. People trading or investing in tips turn out to be one-third of the total losers. What we have to do is make ourselves believe that we can learn and manage our portfolio better by ourselves, and in this way, we can create our own world of wealth creation. Remember that one has to die to see heaven and no one else can do it for him.

This doesn't mean all financial advisers are to be grouped in the category of fraudulent persons as there are many good advisers who apply fundamental knowledge to research about a company and give their honest opinion, and they will try to convince you with a healthy overall portfolio return rather than false expectations of doubling money instantly or alike.

You should think about following an investment adviser only after giving yourself an honest chance to learn and master the art or science of finding multi-bagger stocks and believe me, there is a very sound probability for this. Because if you chose to read this book, then you definitely possess the rare intent, which many losers in the market do not have. Just take a sword in your hand and fight the battle to gain financial freedom.

[8]

"Investing or trading—which means measured risk or higher risk?

There are hardly any traders who managed to become billionaires through returns generated from trading. Taking the experience of others, only investing pertains to be the most dependable source of wealth creation."

[8]

As mentioned earlier, the only way to create enormous wealth from the stock market is to find stocks having the potential to generate multi-bagger returns, invest in them and hold for a sufficiently long duration without being affected by short-term fluctuations. Opposite to this, trading involves purchasing or short-selling stocks with an objective of making gains with short-term ups and downs.

Investing prevails over trading in the following aspects:

1. Investing involves periodic analysis whereas trading involves day-to-day analysis in the case of swing trading, and even minute to minute in the case of intraday analysis. Thus, trading demands a huge devotion of time which is not possible for people with full-time jobs or businesses

2. Investing seems more logical as focus is on the underlying businesses and strengths of

companies. The decision to invest is taken on the basis of sufficient fundamental analysis, whereas trading tends to depend on the sentiments of market players, resulting in temporary ups and downs along with consideration of just one or two fundamental factors. Thus, investing involves measured risks whereas trading involves higher risks

3. Intraday trading, Futures and Options and others are another sort of gambling. Had they been so profitable, there would have been enough examples in the whole world regarding traders who became billionaires by choosing these methods in the stock market. But in reality, there aren't any. People like Warren Buffet or CA Rakesh Jhunjhunwala can be found adopting investment activities and not trading. Though investors like them occasionally engage in swing trading, it is with the limited reason of remaining active with market developments, and the decision to trade in such cases is the by-product arising out of their analysis with regard to main investment activities

SECTION - 2

THE HUNT FOR
MULTI-BAGGER STOCKS

CHAPTER 3

HOW IMPRESSIVE IS THE UNDERLYING BUSINESS AND ITS MANAGEMENT?

[9]

"Companies whose stocks can generate multi-bagger returns run their businesses only upon three things—Economic Moat, Economic Moat and Economic Moat."

[9]

Economic moat (the term popularized by Warren Buffet) means the inherent ability of the business and management of a company to:

- Overcome the performance of its peers (its competitors in the market)

- Thereby maximizing the wealth of shareholders on a consistent basis

- Without any apparent threat to growth in its earnings in the future

Stronger the economic moat, higher are the potential growth opportunities in the company's operations, and higher is the probability of growth in the share price too. This is unavoidable sync. Take it as an iron-magnet combo.

This means the whole story depends on how to know whether a business has economic moat or not. Or say, how to identify businesses running on the basis of economic moat?

Economic moat or competitive advantage can be seen as monopoly power to some extent. Monopoly means the ability of a company to attract more and more customers. This can be possible due to various reasons:

1. Monopoly granted by the government or government entities. Example: Indian railways has given the sole authority to IRCTC Ltd to act as the primary booking agency and to serve as the food caterer to people travelling by train

2. Monopoly granted under any statutory law or enactment

3. Monopoly generated indirectly by the company through the creation of some product differentiation in their products or services or an ability to serve a large variety of customers. Example: Asian Paints, Apple Inc., Havells India Ltd, Tata Consultancy Services Limited, etc.

4. Assurance of returns due to the production of a wide range of products. Example: Hindustan Unilever Ltd

In this world of privatization and fierce competition, there are generally two ways of maintaining competitive advantage or economic moat, which is the third and fourth point above. It means the ability of a business to create product differentiation and customer diversification by providing a wide range of products and services, which is the main reason for maintaining growth prospectus and maximizing shareholders' wealth by providing fabulous returns on their investments. Other types of dominating powers as stated above are also available, but it is not up to such a great level. Companies with any sort of economic moat will have a record of rising business figures year on year along with increasing share prices. This can be evident in any company with a consistent increase in share price over the last three to five years.

How do you judge the availability of economic moat? This question can be answered by the following two approaches:

The first one is **subjective approach.** In this approach, the economic moat is evident in a company by analyzing the following things about it:

- The product differentiation level in the business of a company. This means whether customers prefer this brand over others

- The effectiveness of management

- Supply-demand ratio of products or services provided by the company. This means if the business has a scope of supply in the wake of

> rising demand or if business operations are reaching a saturation level

- Many other factors

There is no unique or specific way to judge if the business of a particular company enjoys economic moat or not. It is clearly evident that any or all the above factors require access to information, which is out of reach of the public at large, and it also requires endless time and energy to attempt to judge all of the above.

The second one is **objective approach.** It is a point to be noted that if a company has a business which enjoys all or any of the economic moat factors mentioned above i.e. it has product differentiation, is governed with effective management or there is adequate supply scope in wake of rising demand, etc., it will have only one thing as a result of all these—rise in profit and financial position, which will clearly be evident from adequate analysis of the financial statements of the company.

In other words, **whether or not a company has economic moat in its business can be answered by undertaking certain analyses of the financial statements of that company for a certain number of preceding years.**

This approach is quite practical, and all the data required for conducting such analyses are available on company websites or on NSE or BSE websites or other online platforms.

Resultantly, only the second option is viable for retail investors.

Fasten your seat belts as we are coming to the most important part of the journey or learning.

[10]

"Purchasing shares of a company is nothing but becoming a partial owner of the business of that company. So behaving like a prospective owner is quite important.

First and foremost, it is required to analyze the financial statements and related documents of the company to find out whether they are doing well in the recent past as a measure of their economic moat."

---

[10]

Suppose you wish to buy a running business offered to you. In this situation, you definitely need to analyze some important elements before deciding whether to invest in that business and become its absolute or partial owner. For answering this question, it is absolutely necessary to evaluate with maximum accuracy the quality of the business, its future growth prospects and the effectiveness of management. The process to evaluate these necessary parameters will mainly involve two stages:

1. The first one is whether the business will be able to generate desired results in the future in terms of increasing profitability and financial position (Screening)

2. The second one is whether the quotation or price charged by the existing owner to sell full or partial ownership in that business is justifiable. It should be justifiable with respect to expected benefits associated with that business in the future (Valuation)

Investing by purchasing the shares of a company is also equal to becoming a partial owner of its business. So both the screening and valuation stages have to be conducted but in a different manner and approach i.e. objective approach.

In the coming parts, we will discuss how various concepts and ratios are employed to judge the following propositions about various companies, their businesses and management in order to consider investment opportunities in them:

- Whether they maintain their profitability year after year

- Whether they are able to increase business and thus their income

- Whether they are able to stand on their own feet i.e. able to rise on their own without excessive borrowings

- What is the image of the company in the eyes of its lenders i.e. capital providers other than owners?

- Whether they are able to provide outstanding returns on their shareholders' funds

- Whether their stocks performed in the near past as a reflection of their strength

All the above-mentioned criteria will be addressed collectively through the process detailed hereby called preliminary screening.

Applying processes to find all the above parameters about each and every company will be a tedious manual process as it requires you to search through the financials and reports of 5000 plus listed companies in India. There is no need to worry about that. We will apply all the required analytical factors with the help of a suitable screener which will simultaneously do a preliminary screening of all the stocks in one go. There are various screeners of stocks available, but I prefer www.screener. in and www.tickertape.in jointly for my analysis. In the next few chapters, we will discuss the various parameters to be checked through the screener, which helps in preliminary screening.

CHAPTER 4

SEVEN CHARACTERISTICS OF A WINNER STOCK—SCREENING OF 5000 PLUS STOCKS

[11]

"Financial statements along with reports and comments issued by auditors and the management, as depicted in the annual report and results issued by a company, contain almost all the information required to perform multibagger analyses. A little glimpse of financial statements may prove helpful in understanding the concepts as we move ahead."

[11]

Financial statements of a listed company comprise of the following parts:

1. Balance Sheet:

   This contains values of assets, liabilities and shareholders' wealth up to a particular date. Assets are shown on one side whereas liabilities and shareholders' funds are shown on the other side of the balance sheet. Also, the values of assets and liabilities are classified as non-current and current. Non-current assets are the assets which will take time beyond one year from the balance sheet date to get converted into cash, whereas current assets are expected to get converted into cash within a year from the balance sheet date.

Non-current liabilities are the obligations of the company which are required or intended to be settled beyond one year from the balance sheet date, whereas current liabilities are required to be paid off within a year from the balance sheet date.

Shareholders' funds comprise of two portions:

➤ The first one is Share Capital, which consists of the amount invested by shareholders in total to run the company

➤ The second one is Other Equity, which consists of the premium charged over the issue of shares by the company to shareholders, reserves created for meeting specified liabilities like the redemption of preference shares, etc. and general reserves containing all the profits generated from running the business as accumulated till the balance sheet date

2. Statement of Profit and Loss A/c:

This contains details of revenue generated, expenses incurred and profits earned in rupee terms and earning per share i.e. EPS. Accumulation of profits earned over the life of a company is the wealth created by the company over and above the invested amount in the form of share capital and is shown under general reserves in the shareholders' wealth portion of the balance sheet.

Apart from this, the profit and loss account also contains important information like earning per share and tax impacts, which are quite important in considering our purchase decision. How? We will discuss the same later.

3. Cash Flow Statement:

This contains information about how the cash is generated and used in running and growing the business. The classification of cash generated and used is shown in three categories:

a. Cash generated/used from operating activities

Amount reported under this section shows how much cash is generated or used by the company for running its ordinary business operations.

b. Cash generated/used from investing activities

Amount reported under this section shows how much cash is generated from selling or disposing its assets and investments and how much cash is used by the company for purchasing assets and other investments.

c. Cash generated/used from financing activities

Amount reported under this section shows how much cash is generated by raising capital from lenders or by issuing fresh share capital and how much cash is used for repayment of money raised by the company from lenders and shareholders.

The information given in the cash flow statement helps analyze how well the company is able to generate cash or cash equivalents while earning profits. Applying some criteria while analyzing the information shown under cash flow statements helps understand whether the company can face liquidity crunch in spite of earning the expected profit from running the business as there may be a possibility that profits could be adequate, but it may be blocked by debtors of the company.

4. Notes to Financial Statements:

In this section, detailed descriptions of all the figures mentioned in the various heads of balance sheet and profit and loss accounts are mentioned, which further helps identify the amounts shown under various heads under financial statements. Example: The balance sheet contains the total amount of properties, plants and equipment held by a company, whereas the detailed note in 'notes to financial statements' section shows the classification of the total amount into each category of assets like land, building, machinery, vehicles, etc.

Furthermore, each listed company issues at the year-end (31st March of every year) and half-year-end

(30th September of every year) a full set of financials consisting of a balance sheet, profit and loss account, cash flow statements and notes to financial statements. However, notes to financial statements are not required for half-year reporting.

Also, for each quarter ending, all listed companies have to announce results from their business operations showing revenue, expenses and income over the quarter along with various comparisons of previous periods. The company also issues a press release after each quarter-end highlighting important aspects of the result and other information.

All the data required for our analysis including financial statements, notes, shareholding patterns, ratio analysis, etc. can be easily found on bseindia.com, moneycontrol.com, investing.com, ratestar.in, screener.in and various other online platforms.

This is all that a person from a non-finance field needs to know about financial statements in order to conduct a multi-bagger analysis. There is no need to know how statements are prepared stage by stage. Know how to drive the vehicle, and forget about its mechanism.

Before conducting the annual general meeting, regarding a particular financial year-end, the company issues an annual report for the concerned financial year, a very significant document which helps understand every aspect a value investor needs. Along with financial data, reports issued by the management, auditors, etc. along with details of the company form a part of the company's annual report. We will discuss in the coming chapters how and to what extent the details shown under financial statements, annual report, results and press releases need to be assessed.

As an example, you can search any stock on Google, the price of which has risen continuously over the last few years and go through that company's financial statements and other details. You will find that some similarities exist in those companies' businesses, which makes their stock price rise continuously. Those similarities are hereby grouped and named as the title of this chapter, 'Seven Characteristics of Winner Stocks'. Let's proceed with the first essential characteristic of stocks which have multi-bagger potential in the next quote. Also, do remember that all these seven factors, forming a part of the screening stage, are to be tested with the help of a screener which will hardly take a few minutes, but it is imperative to know what they actually tell about the business and why it is important to analyze all of them in relation to a company.

Note: Financials to be selected for our analysis should be consolidated and not standalone. In fact, all screeners use consolidated financial statements only for shortlisting or screening. Consolidated financial statements depict the combined picture of all the companies held under the same management, and it is important to analyze them in combination.

[12]

"Factor no. 1 – Revenue Growth with at least 8% annualized rate in the last three years.

Companies having businesses with growth prospects must have a consistent increase in revenue generated over the last few years. Growth in business is a synonym of growth in sales turnover. Simple."

---

[12]

Revenue means the amount derived by selling goods or services in which the company deals. You will agree without any doubt that consistently growing companies availing economic moat, as discussed earlier, will definitely have increased sales figures on a year-to-year basis with some sort of regularity. For screening purpose, we wish to select only those stocks which have an average growth in revenue by 8% on a year-to-year basis over the last three years. In other words, we need to identify the Compounded Annual Growth Rate i.e. CAGR of revenue for the last three years.

The formula for calculating the CAGR (Revenue, three years) is as follows:

CAGR (REV, 3Y) = (Revenue in the latest completed financial year/Revenue in the first year out of three years immediately preceding the last financial year) ^ (1/3) -1

Example: If 2018-19 is the latest completed year, then the first year out of three years preceding 2018-19 (i.e. 2015-16 to 2017-18) will be 2015-16.

Note: Regarding the analysis of the trend of growth in sales and profit, I used to consider growth over the last five years in my recent years of stock market exposure, but adoption of this practice has a chance of eliminating those companies from consideration which grew in the recent past and have a scope of future growth too. So I started considering a shorter period of three years for growth analysis.

Illustrations of the complete analysis using the whole process will be shown at the end of the book after defining all of them.

[13]

"Factor no. 2 – Profit growth with at least 10% annualized rate in the last three years.

Consistent growth in revenue is nothing if profit is not rising enough. Growth in business is a synonym of growth in sales turnover, but growth in wealth maximization of investors is a shadow of growth in profits over the same period."

---

[13]

Profit means the excess revenue generated over expenses incurred in a business over a period. The amount by which shareholders' wealth has increased throughout the life of a company is nothing but the sum total of profits earned by the company in its whole life since its inception till the date of the balance sheet. Not only should the company earn profits each year, but those profits should also rise year by year in order to define a business as having economic moat.

Just increase in revenue won't suffice if the business is not able to generate more profits even after generating more sales year by year. In the same way, increase in profits without an increase in revenue at similar levels won't be a good sign because it will simply mean that the company is able to maintain profits just by controlling and reducing its expenses. This can be a temporary treasure in the hands of the company if it is not able to increase its profit jointly with increase in revenue.

For screening purpose, we wish to select only those stocks which have an average growth in profit by 10% on a year-to-year basis over the last three years. In other words, we need to identify the Compounded Annual Growth Rate i.e. CAGR of profit for the last three years.

The formula for calculating the CAGR (Profit Before Taxes or PBT, three years) is as follows:

CAGR (PBT, 3Y) = (PBT in the latest completed year/ PBT in the first year out of the three years preceding the last completed year) ^ (1/3)-1

Note: We are using profit before tax in place of profit after tax for this analysis because we will test the same at the valuation stage and not screening stage.

[14]

"Factor no. 3 – Return on Equity and Average Return on Equity over the last five years should be at least 15% and 14% respectively.

Companies having raised revenue and profits on a year-to-year basis are welcome, but are they providing enough on the capital invested in them?"

---

[14]

Deeper the power of economic moat inherent in a company, higher is the Return on Equity.

Return on Equity or ROE can be treated as the captain of the seven factors presented in this chapter. Return on Equity refers to earnings made utilizing the amount of shareholders' wealth available to be used by the company throughout the year. In literal terms, Return on Equity means how much is earned utilizing Re 1 of shareholders' funds. ROE reveals directly whether the company is able to generate returns over shareholders' funds, which are substantially higher than riskless investments like fixed deposits or minimal risk investment options like debentures, etc. Hence, this is a measure of the rate at which a company is able to increase the wealth of shareholders in a particular year. One can also treat increasing ROE over the last few years as a synonym of economic moat, provided other factors are also in line.

Example: Suppose you invest Rs 10 lakh to set up a food outlet in the market. You spend on utensils, equipment, interior and other essentials. The performance of the business in the coming three years is as follows:

First Year

Capital at the beginning of the year = 10 lakh

Sales during the year amounts to Rs 8 lakh and the profit earned is Rs 1.5 lakh. This means you earned 1.5 lakh over an investment of Rs 10 lakh during the year. The return on investment earned by the business is 15%, which is significantly more than what you get by investing in a bank's fixed deposit at the rate of say 7%.

Second Year

Capital at the beginning of the year = 10 lakh + 1.5 lakh (profit from the first year) i.e. Rs 11.5 lakh

Sales at the end of the year stated at Rs 10 lakh and the profit earned is Rs 2.5 lakh. This means you earned 2.5 lakh over an investment of Rs 11.5 lakh during the year. The return on investment earned by the business is 21.74% approx., which is also significantly more than fixed deposits' rate.

Third Year

Capital at the beginning of the year = 11.5 lakh + 2.5 lakh (profit from the second year) i.e. Rs 14 lakh

Sales at the end of the year stated at Rs 12 lakh and the profit earned is Rs 3 lakh. This means you earned Rs 3 lakh over an investment of Rs 14 lakh during the year. The return on investment earned by the business is 21.43% approx.

Understanding the journey of the business taken in the example, you get to know why the return on the amount invested by you is important to consider in the initial year as well as the following years. The same holds true while considering the returns made by the company too. The company should be able to utilize the capital of shareholders in such a way that it results in profits at a rate higher than fixed deposit rates.

So what could be more useful for an investor to know? **From the point of view of an investor, ROE is the most useful factor, and it could be the real incarnation of economic moat.**

For our analysis, we will screen those stocks which have Return on Equity greater than or equal to 15% in the latest reported year. Not only this, but the Return on Equity rate should also be maintained on an average for the last five reported years. The minimum average rate of the last five years can be taken as 14% in place of 15% to not avoid selection of stocks, the underlying businesses of which are in improving stage.

The formula for finding Return on Equity is as follows:

ROE = Net Income/Shareholders' Funds*100

Or

Profit After Tax (PAT)/Shareholders' Funds*100

'Net Income' means the profit after taxes generated by the company during the year. 'Shareholders' funds' means the sum of equity share capital and reserves and the surplus of the company or in other words, assets minus liabilities. It is the amount invested in the company's business by shareholders at the beginning of the year.

Note: It is better to consider the criteria of 18% or more for both ROE and average ROE when the market is in bullish mode, while a rate of 15% is acceptable in bearish and normal markets. You need to keep an eye on this when you are doing the analysis.

[15]

"Factor no. 4 – Return on Capital Employed and average Return on Capital Employed over the last five years should be at least 15% and 14% respectively.

It would be well and good if along with adequate returns on investor's capital, the company is also able to generate adequate returns on all sorts of capital, be it owned or borrowed."

---

[15]

Return on Capital Employed or ROCE means the earnings made by the company from the utilization of the whole capital employed in business, be it the net worth of shareholders or borrowed capital. The company must be able to generate returns on the whole capital employed at a rate which surpasses the rate of borrowing on borrowed funds.

ROCE reveals whether the company is able to generate returns which are substantially higher than the borrowing costs incurred, leaving sufficient returns for shareholders after paying off such borrowing costs.

ROCE = EBIT/ (Shareholders' funds + Debt)

Or

Operating profit/Capital employed

The reason why EBIT (Earnings Before Interest and Taxes) is used here in place of net income or PAT, as in the case of ROE, is that while calculating returns on the capital employed, the returns or earnings taken should be the amount generated for both shareholders' funds and borrowed funds together. PAT is used while calculating Return on Equity because PAT is the amount available solely for equity holders after meeting all the expenses and taxes, including interest on borrowed funds, and that is what matters while calculating Return on Equity.

The significance of calculating and checking ROCE is to find out whether the capital structure i.e. combination of equity and debt employed by the company in its business is suitable or not. In the case of excessive debt, the ROCE will become substantially lower than ROE because ROCE is calculated by taking both debt and equity in the denominator. So a low ROCE is not good for shareholders because it will eat up their wealth by ultimately lowering the ROE. This is because excessive borrowing will result in declining net profit margins due to increased borrowing costs in the current year and coming years.

Suppose in the example used above, you invested Rs 8 lakh initially from your pocket and Rs 2 lakh through borrowings. Then the picture could be:

First Year

Owner's capital at the beginning = 8 lakh

Borrowed funds = 2 lakh

Total capital employed = 10 lakh

Sales during the year amounts to Rs 8 lakh and the profit earned is Rs 1.5 lakh. Apart from this, the interest paid on borrowings is Rs 28,000 or Rs 0.28 lakh. Then the figures of ROCE and ROE will be:

ROCE = 1.5 lakh/10 lakh means 18.75%

Net Profits = 1.5 lakh - 0.28 lakh i.e. 1.22 lakh

ROE = 1.22 lakh/8 lakh i.e. 15.25%

Second Year

Owner's capital at the beginning = 9.22 lakh

Borrowed funds = 2.00 lakh

Total capital employed = 11.22 lakh

Sales during the year amounts to Rs 10 lakh and the profit earned is Rs 2.5 lakh. Apart from this, the interest paid on borrowings is Rs 28,000 or Rs 0.28 lakh. Then the figures of ROCE and ROE will be:

ROCE = 2.5 lakh/11.22 lakh means 22.28%

Net Profits = 2.5 lakh - 0.28 lakh i.e. 2.22 lakh

ROE = 2.22 lakh/9.22 lakh i.e. 24.08%

Third Year

Owner's capital at the beginning = 11.44 lakh

Borrowed funds = 2.00 lakh

Total capital employed = 13.44 lakh

Sales during the year amounts to Rs 12 lakh and the profit earned is Rs 3 lakh. Apart from this, the interest paid on borrowings is Rs 28,000 or Rs 0.28 lakh. Then the figures of ROCE and ROE will be:

ROCE = 3 lakh/13.44 lakh means 22.32%

Net Profits = 3 lakh - 0.28 lakh i.e. 2.72 lakh

ROE = 2.72 lakh/11.44 lakh i.e. 23.77%

In the above example, both the ROCE and ROE are quite healthy, and it can be said that the business is able to utilize the combined debt and equity capital in a very good manner. In fact, the ROE generated is better as compared to when borrowed funds were not involved in the capital structure of the company.

Hence, if the company is availing a healthy capital structure, its ROCE will be above 15%. And for the purpose of taking the average of the last three years, we will opt for the rate of 14 %.

[16]

"Factor no. 5 – Pledging of promoter's shares is generally slow poison for a company. It would be divine for companies to avoid this. But sometimes, when circumstances govern, a little quantity of venom acts as a medicine for the treatment of some disease. Hence, there should not be pledging of shares by promoters in excess of 10% of their total holding.

Indication that lenders are having any sort of doubt over the capacity of the company to repay their dues is not positive. Not finding a company's circumstances viable for taking more borrowings and demanding to pledge their shares for raising more loans is not good."

---

[16]

Pledging of shares is a certain kind of mortgage given by promoters to banks or financial institutions to borrow money. In the event that the company is not able to repay the principal or interest component of the loan, the lender is authorized to sell the pledged holdings of promoters in the open market to recover the amount remaining unpaid. Pledging of own shares is required by the promoters of a company when the amount which the company intends to borrow is too big to be freely allowed by lending organizations. This is because in the opinion of lenders, there is some sort of probability that the company's business may not be able to generate enough profits or maintain enough liquidity, and this may prevent the company from clearing its dues timely in the future. Generally, pledging conditions are insisted by lending organizations when a company borrows excessive debts or because there may be some kind of risk to future business operations of the borrowing company.

Even if the company has growth prospects well enough for considering it as an investment alternative, pledging of its promoter's holdings can create a future risk of selling promoter's shares in the event that the company is unable to generate enough returns to pay its dues timely. In that case, lenders may sell the promoter's holdings and recover that amount. If the pledging ratio is high, this will eventually lead to lowering of promoter's holding in the business by a substantial proportion. Sudden reduction in the promoter's shareholding in a company leads to a sudden decline in the price of the company's share.

However, in order to explore a little beyond the boundaries of a company's existing business levels, sometimes a limited portion of pledging is opted to raise a little extra borrowing. This is chosen by a company as part of the measured risk in their hands so that they can level up their operations, which means increase them in a significant manner, and that could not have been possible with the borrowing available freely.

Though it would be best if a company has nil promoter's pledging ratio, if all other factors are impressive, it is sometimes favourable to accept pledging ratio up to a limit of 10% to take investment decisions.

Also note that for preliminary screening, we will select candidates with a pledging ratio not exceeding 10%. But after applying the valuation stage, if there are enough number of good candidates left, we will select only those which either have nil pledging ratio or quite lesser than 10%.

[17]

"Factor no. 6 – Debt to Equity ratio should be up to 1 or 100%. In case the industry in which the company operates has a common practice of maintaining Debt to Equity ratio beyond 1, then it is maintainable but not beyond 1.5 or 150% in any case.

Debt is not dangerous. But dangerous is its excess. Borrowing should not be at a level that creates pressure on the management for timely repayment of dues."

---

[17]

A company has debt in its capital structure. This means the company utilizes the funds raised by borrowing from banks or others for maintaining its operations and growth. Debt is not dangerous at all. Why? Let's understand. Suppose a company has Return on Capital Employed at 25% and avails bank finance at the rate of 14%. What does this signify? It signifies that the company is earning 25% over whatever money it borrowed from the bank and used it for the purpose of business, whereas for use of that money, it needs to pay to the bank a mere 14% upon it. This means the company made a profit of 11% over that borrowed money and that profit will be added to the wealth of shareholders. This benefit is referred to as leverage benefit in the finance world.

But everything beyond a limit is void and harmful. When a company brings borrowed fund into its capital structure to support its business growth, it undertakes a risk of repaying a definite amount in the form of interest and principal to the lending bank. This risk may become an unavoidable hurdle for the company when it is not able to generate sufficient returns to repay the loan taken and interest thereon. This may be an obvious situation if the company engages in borrowing excessive debt funds and may even lead it to bankruptcy, thereby affecting shareholders' worth.

Debt is an important part of the financial structure as it helps emerging businesses in a faster way, provided its management is able to deploy the borrowed money with utmost care and prudence to increase the earnings in a good manner. But if the debt component overlaps equity in the capital structure of a company, then a severe problem starts. The problem can be understood in a practical manner as follows:

Let's have in examples the income and expenses of A Ltd and B Ltd.

Income and Expenses of A Ltd and B Ltd		
	A Ltd	**B Ltd**
Total Revenue (A)	1,00,000	70,000
Expenses:		
Operating expenses	40,000	28,000
Employee Benefit expenses	11,000	7,700
Administrative expenses	30,000	21,000
Finance Cost – Interest on borrowings	15,000	2,500
Total Expenses (B)	96,000	59,200
Gross Income (A-B)	4,000	10,800

As evident in the example above, A Ltd has a higher revenue than B Ltd and their expenses are also proportionate with respect to revenue. The only difference lies in the finance cost proportion. A Ltd has a higher finance cost in comparison to B Ltd, which is surely due to excessive borrowings. This results in a comparatively lower profit for A Ltd despite having a higher revenue than B Ltd. Thus, if the business of a company is running on excessive debt, then the interest on borrowings may eat up a good portion of the company's earnings. Had the expenses on debt been only Rs 5,000 in place of Rs 15,000, A Ltd would have a profit of Rs 14,000 which is 14% of its revenue but actually, it is only Rs 4,000 i.e. 4% of the total revenue.

What difference does this create? B Ltd is left with Rs 10,800 as Return over Equity whereas A Ltd has only Rs 4,000 in that particular period.

Let's assume B Ltd earns at the rate of 15% over the net worth of shareholders on a compounding basis for the next 10 years, whereas let's take the same rate as 10% for A Ltd because due to their excessive borrowings, they will incur more cost year after year and therefore their Return on Equity cannot be as good as B Ltd, provided other things remain the same.

By utilizing the current year's profit of Rs 10,800, B Ltd will have the compounded amount at the end of 10 years as $10,800*(1+15\%)^{10}$ which equals Rs 43,692/-

However, in the hands of A Ltd, the amount of Rs 4,000 will grow for the next 10 years at the compounding rate of 10% which is $4,000*(1+10\%)^{10}$ resulting in Rs 10,375/-

It is clearly noticeable that excessive debt not only results in lesser profit in the current year but also impacts future wealth creation for shareholders of the company. Hence, it is important to consider Debt to Equity ratio before investing in a stock as it judges the ability of the company to pay back the funds borrowed along with due interest. Debt to Equity ratio makes this judgement possible.

This equals the total liabilities of the company divided by shareholders' funds.

$$\text{Debt to Equity ratio} = \frac{\text{Total Debt}}{\text{Shareholders' funds.}}$$

Here 'Total Debt' includes long-term liabilities in the form of loans plus a portion of long-term loans (non-current liabilities) which have to be paid within a year and disclosed under the heading short-term liabilities (current liabilities) in the balance sheet.

The ideal ratio for the purpose of investing in the long run should be 1:1 or 1 or 100%. This will ensure there are lesser chances of a company being endangered with the risk of bankruptcy in the future. However, as said before, it is maintainable up to 1.5 if this is the industry practice and other factors are quite satisfactory.

Note:

1. The Debt-Equity ratio is not useful while analyzing banking sector stocks. How? We will discuss this in a specific chapter waiting ahead.

2. I personally do not consider stocks with Debt to Equity ratio above 1 or 100% because every time I conduct my research, I have enough options. So I do not feel the need to go for shares with a DE ratio of 1 to 1.5 on a conservative note.

[18]

"Factor no. 7 or the 7th Sense – Even when all other factors are satisfactory, the share price of the company should have given positive returns in the last one year and at least 30% in the last three years.

A tiger kept in a cage for long is the same as a cat. It can't hunt. Even with increasing business and wealth of shareholders, if a stock is not able to generate enough returns over its market price in the last few years, then it is doubtful if it will do the same in the future too."

---

[18]

Limited access to information about a company and its operations is what retail investors are destined to. They may access all the information made freely available by the company, including its financial statements, reports and others declared by the company, but not beyond that. It is possible to identify the fulfilment of other factors through easily accessible information. But in rare cases, it is also possible that some invisible disturbing element(s) may exist in the company, which may result in lowering of share price in the coming future. And those negative elements are not clearly visible to outsiders.

With the available information, one can judge the other six factors, but this seventh factor i.e. the Seventh Sense, can be satisfied and revealed in a clear manner through the price chart of the company's shares. Just imagine if a company is able to:

- increase its revenue and profit by 8-10% or above annually over the last three years

- maintain Debt to Equity ratio within 1 or 1.5, as the case may be

- maintain average ROE and ROCE over the last three years as 15% or more

- sustain pledging of promoter's holdings below 10% of their total holdings

Then how is its stock not able to provide returns by at least 10% simple interest rate over the last three years?

As a strict rule,

In the last three years, the price of the stock should have risen by at least 30%. We are considering the return on stock price over the last three years because we need to observe the performance of a company's stock throughout the period we are considering for growth in revenue and profits. Apart from this, we also need to check if the return on share price over the last 12 months is at least positive. It is necessary to have the last one-year return as positive, even when the share price has increased by 30% in the last three years because if a company has been affected by some negative elements in recent times, this will help eliminate such stocks from our subsequent analysis i.e. valuation stage. It is better to focus on stocks which have a higher probability of becoming multi-bagger stocks rather than stocks which have ambiguity in their underlying business.

Note: Often screeners provide data for change in price only for the last one year and not for three years. In that case, you can filter the stock with one-year price change being positive and the three years criteria can be manually checked for any company on Google at the time of valuation analysis, which will come after the preliminary checking.

[19]

"Applying the seven factors of preliminary screening will bring the list of 5000 plus stocks listed on stock exchanges to a final list of 50-70 potential stocks, which is a necessary input for the valuation stage.

After confirming that a business is fruitful with enough growth opportunities in the coming future, the next stage is to ensure that the consideration charged for acquiring that business or a portion of that business is not more than the benefits which will be fetched by that business in the future over investment value of the buyer."

[19]

Valuation of a business is a paramount factor in deciding to buy that business either fully or partially. Buying silver at the price of gold can never be acceptable. A similar concept applies while buying a stock too. You need to calculate the fair price with reference to a stock as per the conditions of that company's operations and future growth prospects by applying further tests. It should not be considered as an investment opportunity if the current price of the stock is running above that fair price. For valuation, we will use the list of stocks obtained after preliminary analysis as input. Apart from this, in the valuation stage, we will also observe other factors manually about shortlisted companies to ensure they do not suffer from any other limitations which may harm business operations or share prices in the near future.

CHAPTER 5

WILL WINNERS WIN IN THE FUTURE TOO? – VALUATION

[20]

"Upon getting the final list of potential candidates, each one of them has to be checked again to ensure there are no hidden defects in them. The analysis will be done taking the combined inputs of financial statements and other information of a company for the last few years."

[20]

For undertaking pre-valuation analysis, as mentioned here, one needs to first obtain financial statements for five years on a comparative basis. This will include all three components of financial statements i.e. balance sheet, profit and loss account and cash flow statements for five years to compare. The information can be easily accessed on screener.in, moneycontrol.com, investing. com, tickertape.in, etc. I prefer screener.in for my analysis. Also, some sites allow you to download the desired information in Excel format.

After obtaining all the desired information on the screen, perform the following steps:

1. **Is the company able to convert an adequate proportion of its profits into cash and cash equivalents?**

   Step 1: Obtain from cash flow statements the sum of cash flow from operating activities for the last five completed years.

   Step 2: Obtain from profit and loss accounts the sum of profit after taxes for the last five completed years.

   Step 3: Compare the results obtained from Step 1 with Step 2. The sum of cash flow should at least be 75% of the sum of net profit after tax for the last five years.

   If profits are the fuel of the business, then cash is the engine oil. Both are necessary to drive the company towards success. Hence, the company should be able to generate at least 75% of its profits in cash. This will ensure the company does not face any cash crunch in the near future and that a huge portion of the company's profits is not blocked in debtors or trade receivables. It ensures that the company regularly realizes cash with respect to sales made to customers. For a more conservative approach, we can take 80% criteria in place of 75% i.e. the sum of cash flow from operations should at least be 75% to 80% of the sum of profit after taxes for the last five years. **This is called the CFO/ Profit test.** More the ratio stands above 80%, it is better.

Note: This analysis is of no use for banking stocks as their financial statements, including cash flow statements, are prepared in a different manner from other stocks, and the above criteria won't be satisfied even when the banking company is good. How to conduct an analysis of banking stocks is mentioned in a specific chapter ahead.

2. **Is the company reporting tax impacts in profit and loss accounts close to the tax rate applicable?**

For a company, the applicable tax rate is around 25% and 33% as per their selection of tax rates. Thus, the following steps need to be taken to judge this condition:

Step 1: Calculate the percentage of 'tax' over 'profit before tax' with respect to the last five years, which is called as 'effective tax rate'.

Step 2: Calculate the average of the effective tax rates for the last five years.

The resultant percentage figure should approximately be in the range of 25% to 36%.

In case the company reports an average tax rate much lower than 25% of profit before tax, then this is a sign of caution. This entails that further analysis is required to know the reason behind the same.

Example: A company may choose to claim certain tax incentives, but these tax incentives may not last long. Hence, in the future, when tax incentives are not available, then the tax impacts will rise, which will lower the profit after tax and even earning per share. This could probably lower the share price of the company considering this scenario. Hence, it is better to either avoid companies which show lesser average than tax rates. If one wants to invest still, then the reason must be obtained by digging further into the annual report of the company for the respective years. The desired information can be fetched from the respective note in Notes to Accounts showing reconciliation of tax over accounting profits and actual tax liability being charged to profit and loss account.

3. **Does the company possess a continuous commitment to growth?**

This can be ensured by observing whether revenue, profits and earning per share have grown in the last five years on a continuous basis with some sort of consistency. Hence, in comparative statements of profit and loss for the last three to five years, the following are to be observed:

a. Whether revenue in the last three to five years has increased year by year

b. Whether net profit (PAT) in the last three to five years has increased year by year

c. Whether Diluted EPS in the last three to five years has increased year by year

There may be some instances where revenue and net profits are increasing but EPS is not increasing on the same scale. The reason behind that must be identified. If this is due to the issue of bonus shares in any year or due to raising further capital, then it is acceptable.

4. **Is Return on Equity free from unnecessary risk elements? – DuPont Analysis**

As per the third factor of screening, Return on Equity should be above 15% for prima facie selection of stocks with multi-bagger potential. Furthermore, post-mortem of Return on Equity can even state whether the company would be able to sustain the Return on Equity in the coming years with the same effect. This analysis is called DuPont Analysis.

Post-mortem means the division of ratio of Return on Equity into three portions:

1. Operating efficiency: This means profit earned over each rupee of sales i.e. PAT/Gross Revenue

2. Asset utilization efficiency: This means revenue generated over each rupee of total assets available with the company i.e. Gross Revenue/Total Assets

3. Equity multiplier: This means indirectly getting an idea of how much debt is used by the company to finance its assets i.e. Total Assets/Equity

Hence,

Return on Equity = PAT/Gross Revenue

        X Gross Revenue/Total Assets

        X Total Assets/Equity

(Or)

Return on Equity = PAT/Equity

Operating efficiency, the first component of Return on Equity, is the absolute measure of the profitability of a company's business. The higher it is, the better.

Asset utilization efficiency, the second measure, is a measure of effectiveness in the use of assets by the company to generate revenue. The higher it is, the better. This is not useful for professional companies as the number of tangible assets held is quite small.

Equity multiplier or financial leverage ratio, the final measure of ROE, entails in an indirect manner the extent to which the company's assets are funded by borrowed money. Not using leverage may put the company at a disadvantageous position as compared to peers in the industry, but using excessive debt can create a disproportionate risk. Now since financial leverage is a component of ROE, higher the financial leverage, higher the ROE. But will that be a good indication even if the company avails excessive debt? Definitely not. Hence, if the increase in ROE is due to increase in financial leverage beyond a tolerable point, we will not put that stock on priority while making an investment decision. The ideal financial leverage ratio stands as:

- **4**, if the company's CFO/PAT ratio, as mentioned earlier, is between 0.75 to 1
- **5**, if the CFO/PAT ratio is above 1

One thing to be kept in mind is that the company has to satisfy the above-mentioned criteria for the last completed year and the average of equity multipliers for the last five years should be within the above-mentioned limits. This is really important to judge how the company maintains its strength. In other words, the equity multiplier for the last five years has to be calculated in Excel and their average should be within the above-mentioned limits.

Note:

1. This situation will rarely arise because the Debt to Equity ratio is already being tested at the preliminary screening stage, which will eliminate companies funded with excessive debt. **But then, it is better to confirm from a different angle.**

2. The Du Pont analysis won't work on banking sector stocks.

[21]

"First element of valuation: P/E Ratio i.e. Price-Earnings Ratio—the figure bundled with many hidden truths.

What price is demanded by an investor to earn Re 1 in the company at present is an important question."

---

[21]

Price-Earnings Ratio, P/E Ratio, means multiple in which the current price of the share of a company stands with respect to earning per share of that company during the last completed year or 12 trailing months. This ratio states how much price a share will cost with respect to Re 1 earned by the company. Or in other words, P/E Ratio determines what you need to pay to earn one rupee in that company. The formula to calculate P/E is as follows:

P/E Ratio = CMP of share/EPS of share

Here,

- CMP means Current Market Price of share i.e. the price at which the share is available at this moment

- EPS to calculate P/E Ratio means EPS of the company for the last 12 months from the date when the company last reported its results. This is because every listed company discloses its results each quarter and the period of 12 months ending the last reported quarter is to be taken into consideration for the calculation of EPS

  Example: If P/E is to be calculated in April or May, then the EPS of 12 months ending last March result is to be taken.

  If P/E is calculated in July, then the EPS of 12 months ending last June results of the company will be taken and so on. This will make sure you use the latest data while considering investment decisions.

Apparently, the lesser the PE, the better it is. This is because you need to pay a lesser amount to have the same earnings in the future. In the case of growing companies, the earnings will rise so the price of the stock will also rise in order to keep the P/E at an adequate level. Now read and understand very carefully as this is the knowledge which makes the difference between profitable and non-profitable investments.

Facts about P/E Ratio:

- P/E Ratio determines what investors presume about the company in the future. If investors believe that a company will grow at a good pace in the future, they will accept to pay more to earn one rupee in that company. It means they will be ready to purchase stock at a greater P/E. Hence, healthy P/E means investors have a good perception of the company's growth in the future.

  But this doesn't mean we should simply invest in companies when their P/E has risen.

- P/E Ratio often signifies whether the stock is overpriced or not. Suppose a company is growing consistently. Suddenly, many investors get attracted to that stock, creating bulk investments in it. In this situation, the price will go up significantly because the market price is a game of demand and supply. This can make the stock overpriced too.

But this also doesn't mean we should simply invest in companies when their P/E is low.

So what does this mean? Both the statements mentioned above are contradicting, which means they are opposite to each other. This means we need to use P/E Ratio only as an input to make a decision and not as the ultimate factor for purchase decisions. How? We will discuss in the coming pages.

[22]

"Second element of valuation: Growth Ratio of EPS i.e. Average EPS growth rate over the last three years—the most related factor of a company's growth in terms of rise in shareholders' earnings.

At what rate the shareholders' earnings has risen over a period is the deciding factor for what price a company's share deserves."

---

[22]

What would be the value creation for shareholders ultimately in a company's operations? It would definitely be what the company leaves in the hands of shareholders after paying all the expenses and taxes from revenue i.e. Profit after Tax. The most relevant factor will be profit after tax earned per share or simply earning per share (EPS).

EPS is what finally matters when it comes to measuring a company's growth for shareholders' benefit, provided all other factors discussed so far depict a positive image. The company not only has to earn a profit which belongs only to shareholders, but it also has to provide incremental profits year after year to prove that the company is growing in real terms. Thus, for this purpose, we will calculate the average growth in earning per share of the company for the last three completed years. The formula for calculation of average growth rate of EPS is:

G, Average Growth Rate of EPS (in terms of %) =

$$1/3 \text{ x } 100 \text{ x } (\text{EPS Year}^1 / \text{EPS Year}^0$$
$$+\text{EPS Year}^2 / \text{EPS Year}^1$$
$$+\text{EPS Year}^3 / \text{EPS Year}^2)$$

Where,

EPS Year^0 is EPS of base year. E.g. FY 2015-16

EPS Year^1 is EPS of 1st year. E.g. FY 2016-17

EPS Year^2 is EPS of 2nd year. E.g. FY 2017-18

EPS Year^3 is EPS of 3rd year. E.g. FY 2018-19

Calculating the average growth rate of EPS, we come to know about how the company is able to increase its earnings for shareholders in the recent past. This not only indicates growth but is a very useful factor along with P/E for making a decision regarding whether to purchase a stock which passed preliminary and subsequent stages.

Note:

1. To calculate the correct result, if decline in EPS is due to bonus issue or division of shares, then we

need to eliminate its effect by calculating the EPS of preceding years on the basis of the number of total shares in the most recent year i.e. by dividing the respective year's Profit after Tax with the current total number of shares. Idea of any such event can be seen if EPS declines even when the total share capital remains the same and profits also rise.

2. If rise in EPS is due to the buyback or consolidation of shares, then the effect of the same is to be excluded by calculating the EPS of earlier years by dividing Profit after Tax of those respective years with the current total number of shares.

   Note: The situation will not arise if your source website, from which you extract analytical data, adjusts the EPS as per the current number of shares.

3. If the analysis is done at a time when the recent quarter ending result period was not March i.e. other than at the release of fourth-quarter results, the EPS of running part of the year is to be compared in total with the corresponding period of the immediately completed preceding year. There should be a symbol of growth in that portion of year too.

   Example: If the analysis is done in December 2019, then the average growth of EPS will be calculated as per the above formula after taking into account the following completed years' EPSs:

   EPS of base year i.e. FY 2015-16

   EPS of 1st year i.e. FY 2016-17

EPS of 2nd year i.e. FY 2017-18

EPS of 3rd year i.e. FY 2018-19

In addition to that, one more thing is to be confirmed which is,

EPS of FY 2019-20, up to the last declared result period i.e. from April 2019 to September 2019, is also to be calculated. After that, the same is to be compared to the EPS of the corresponding period of the last financial year i.e. from April 2018 to September 2018.

Suppose,

EPS of FY 2015-16   = 9.25

EPS of FY 2016-17   = 11.10

EPS of FY 2017-18   = 12.57

EPS of FY 2018-19   = 15.26

EPS of April 2018 to September 2018 = 7.64

EPS of April 2019 to September 2020 = 8.42

It is observed that the EPS is rising each year. And when it is further analyzed, the EPS from April 2019 to September 2019 is more than that from April 2018 to September 2018. This ensures that the EPS is rising in the current year too. That is a good indication.

Keep in mind that if this sign is not present, then it is considered that the EPS has touched the saturation point and we will not touch that stock till the time the company again starts generating higher EPS than in the past.

[23]

"PEG Ratio i.e. Price Earning-Growth Ratio—the final and most useful parameter to judge the fairness of a stock's price.

Whether the price of a stock is at par with growth in the earnings of the company on an annual basis is the most important question."

---

[23]

PEG Ratio answers directly whether to invest in a company's share at the current price or not. PEG Ratio has two components: Price-Earnings Ratio and Growth Ratio, which are the first and second elements of valuation analysis respectively as discussed before.

Price-Earnings Ratio determines what price is charged for a stock to provide an earning of Re 1 over that stock.

Growth Ratio determines the average growth in EPS over the last three years.

Is the current market price correct? Does the price have scope to increase after I buy this share at this price? Is there some sort of surety that the stock will not fall down measurably or significantly after I buy at this price? Is it right to pay the price demanded to earn Re 1 in terms of current P/E?

The answer to all these questions lies in a perfect combo of the above-mentioned two elements i.e. P/E Ratio and Growth Ratio. The combo will be in the form of PEG Ratio which is calculated as follows:

PEG Ratio = P/E Ratio of company/Growth Ratio of EPS.

Both the elements used will have to be calculated in the same way as demonstrated in the last two points. One thing to be noted is that P/E Ratio will be in absolute terms whereas Growth Ratio will be in percentage terms. Suppose if P/E Ratio is 15 and Growth Ratio of stock is 10%, then PEG Ratio will be 1.5 i.e. 15/10 and not 15/0.1. Some of my students-cum-friends got that doubt in this instance. I do not want that doubt to arise in the mind of readers.

PEG Ratio will connect the rationale of the price charged for stock with the average growth in EPS of the company and entails at what times the price stands in support of its Growth Ratio.

Now the question that comes to mind is - What picture does this ratio bring to us?

This brings to us the measure of how many multiples of a company's earnings can be accepted as the price of that stock to invest when it rises with a certain percentage of growth.

By comparing the two inputs of PEG Ratio i.e. P/E Ratio and Growth Ratio with each other, an investor understands what P/E Ratio we should accept for a stock if that company has growth in its EPS at say 10%. Ideally 10? Or in other words, you should accept PE of 10 or less for a company which grows by 10%.

Example: If a company is growing its EPS year on year by 10% and its current P/E Ratio is 12, then the acceptable price at P/E of 10 should be 12*10 i.e. 120.

This is because if

P/E Ratio = CMP/EPS of stock

Then

CMP   = P/E Ratio x EPS of stock

The most ideal PEG Ratio will be up to 1 because if a company is growing in terms of EPS at the rate of 10% on a yearly basis, then it is acceptable to have 10 as its P/E Ratio i.e. we can purchase that stock at a price which is not more than 10 times of its latest 12 months trailing EPS.

But apart from this, I also observed another thing throughout my career. This is when a company complies with all other factors of growth as mentioned so far in this book—their stock price moves consistently in the positive direction and such growth in share price pushes the PEG Ratio beyond the most ideal limit of 1 as stated above. But still, the price keeps moving in an upward direction even after that. Examples of this are MRF Ltd, TCS Ltd, etc.

The rationale behind this behaviour of price is very obvious. If a company is running very high potential businesses, then it will attract many investors back to back because all sincere investors who analyze stocks get access to the information and use screeners to search for a potential growth stock. So the PEG Ratio of potentially good companies also often remains above one at many times. This is not at all a bad sign as attraction from more and more buyers in a potentially good business is what keeps the price growing consistently in the long term. Hence, there is no point in avoiding a stock which:

> Is potentially good in terms of growth after due analysis of all the necessary factors as discussed till now

> It has a PEG Ratio slightly above 1

But one more thing to focus upon is that investors can't accept PEG Ratio as anything above 1. Because as said earlier, don't ever buy a good company's stock at a bad price. You need to keep a condition for that to not be more than two.

Yes, this is a rule of thumb to be followed in every case. After analyzing all other factors, finally, it is to be ensured that **the PEG Ratio of a stock should not be more than 2.**

In other words, the most ideal situation should be that the P/E Ratio of a stock should not be more than **two times** its percentage average growth in EPS over the last three years. Following this strictly will avoid the purchase of any shares in an overpriced scenario. After this final confirmation, one can go ahead to buy that particular stock. But do not just conclude with all the things up to here. Just continue reading. There are important facts waiting ahead too.

CHAPTER 6

CHANGES IN SHAREHOLDING PATTERN – SOMETIMES GOOD, SOMETIMES BAD

[24]

"Shareholding pattern changes—just remember a few rules.

You are going to become a small partial owner. So observing how big owners and major players treat the stock is a fire test before choosing the final team of candidates."

[24]

After your preliminary screening is done, when you begin to do the valuation analysis, the analysis of shareholding patterns simultaneously may either take you to the hidden treasure or make you aware of hidden threats. Let's go ahead.

There are four categories of investors in any company:

1. **Promoters and Group:** The faces behind the company's existence. They incorporated the

company and generally hold a major or substantial portion of the company's share size. The shares held by them and their related persons come under this group.

2. **Foreign Institutional Investors and Domestic Institutional Investors:** These include banks, mutual funds, money managers, insurance companies, etc.

3. **Major Public Shareholders:** Corporates and individuals other than those included in the above categories holding more than 1% of the total share capital.

4. **Retail Investors:** Small investors (individuals or others) other than those included in the above categories.

As factors of preliminary screening are already applied, it is in good practice to try to know how promoters and big market players like institutional investors treat the stock.

See, it is obvious that as a small shareholder, if you are going to buy the stock for a gain in the near future, promoters and institutional investors should also see the same potential in the stock of the company. If they have a good interpretation of the stock, they will either

- Increase their holdings

- At least maintain their holdings in total

- At least do not sell a substantial portion in such a way that retail holdings in stock rise by a considerable margin

The company has to declare the shareholding pattern after each quarter-end. Apart from this, details of any block deals between promoters and others or between any third parties also have to be submitted by the company. Such details as declared with respect to shareholding patterns by the company are readily available on BSE or NSE sites and many other online platforms like moneycontrol.com, investing.com, etc. It is imperative for you to access such platforms to obtain information regarding any changes in shareholding patterns of the company as compared to the preceding period(s). Any changes in shareholding patterns will indicate the following mixed signs:

1. **Changes in shareholding pattern depicting positive indications:**

   ➢ Promoters increase their stake from open market purchase – Promoters are the best persons in terms of their knowledge about the business of their company. Why they will increase their stake in the company? They will increase only when they have some strong reason to believe that the stock price may rise in the near future. This indication is quite good and even its validity rises to a great extent when this thing occurs in companies whose businesses pass all the tests of preliminary screening, proving that the business and management together possess economic moat and its stock has multi-bagger potential. The business already shows signs of economic moat and promoters increase their holding too. Isn't it a good sign to rely upon? It is, of course. The business has economic moat, the stock is not overvalued, the current valuation is also satisfactory in comparison to the average over the last couple of years, and promoters are also buying back their shares. What else to wait for? Generally, this exercise of increasing stake is undertaken by promoters during a slowdown or recession in the market.

➤ FIIs and DIIs increase their stake through any means – Why is this a good indication? Institutional investors are banks, mutual funds, money managers, etc. They usually consider stocks for bulk investment after conducting a deep analysis of various factors and after getting satisfied or confident with future business growth prospects and hopeful rise in the stock price in the near future. Their entry in stocks is always positively welcomed and often results in a rise in stock price.

➤ Institutional investors can increase their stake in a company by purchasing from the open market or from promoters or through Qualified Institutional Placement by companies directly. QIP is a process through which a company directly issues its shares to DIIs or FIIs.

➤ As said earlier, a retail investor is destined to limited information about a company, industry and economy which is declared by the company or various other sources within the economy for use of the general public. On the other hand, institutional investors have in-depth experience in the analysis of the fundamentals of any company and also, they are armed with ample information about the economy as a whole, the industry and the company. This makes them take the investment decision in a more prudent manner.

➤ Promoters reducing their stake by selling partial holdings to institutional investors – Promoters reducing their stake can also be positive if the stake sold off is purchased by institutional investors. This only means that the stake is sold off just to fund some need of the promoter and the entry of institutional investors is itself a good sign.

➤ Holding percentage of retail shareholders declines due to an increase in the stake of promoters or institutional investors.

2. **Changes in shareholding pattern depicting negative indications:**

➤ Promoters decreasing their stake continuously by selling in the open market – Promoters continuously reducing their stake gradually through the last few quarters or in a huge percentage i.e. more than 3% in the last one quarter itself by directly selling to retail investors. This is not a good sign as selling stake to retail investors directly on a continuous note simply means that institutional investors are not interested in increasing their holdings in the stock. The situation of the company may indicate either temporary or permanent stoppage in the growth of the company. This may obviously result in fall in share price too.

➤ Combined holdings of DII and FII decline by directly selling in the open market to retail investors – Institutional investors may sell their shares either for compliance with some regulations or as a reflection of their reducing trust in the growth prospects of the company. If substantial selling of their holding i.e. more than 3% only reflects an increase in shareholdings of retail investors (institutional investors do not sell whole or part of their holdings to promoters but wholly to retail investors), then the situation demands caution to be taken by retail investors. This is because whatever be the reason of selling by institutional investors, it may result in a decline in price in the near term.

➤ Continuous rise in holding of retail investors – Increase in holdings of retail investors in the company in a substantial manner and on a continuous note is often enough to prove the company's stock as a trap.

Combined Analytical Note:

After preliminary screening and valuation analysis, the list of all the stocks as shortlisted, along with all other parameters, will probably be in an Excel sheet. In that data, add one more column against the shortlisted shares. The heading of the column would be 'Combined increase (or decrease) in holdings of promoters and institutional investors'. Mention the change in shareholding in the descending order i.e. the stock in which the combined holdings of promoters and institutional investors has risen the most will be at the top. We will discuss how to use this data later in the book.

Note:

1. For saving time, this information of increase in shareholdings of promoters and institutional investors in the last three months can be added as a filter while doing preliminary screening itself and the data is downloaded along with these columns. After valuation analysis, the combined analysis as mentioned above can be performed with great ease.

2. As said earlier, the pledging of promoter's holding should not be in excess of 10% of their holdings.

3. Don't think of change in shareholdings as the sole criteria to take an investment decision. You may have thought at this moment that it is a great shortcut to pick stocks in which promoters or FIIs or DIIs are increasing stake. You will invest over their decision of raising stake, but you wouldn't get the timely

information about their exit, and in that situation, you may end up having a loss over the period of time in your investment because you won't be able to exit timely due to the lack of information.

CHAPTER 7

WHAT MAKES THE MARKET PRICE OF A STOCK MOVE UP?

[25]

"Growing business of a company and the rising price of its stock

Deteriorating business of a company and decline in the price of its stock

– Both are iron-magnet combos.

If the iron-magnet combo is missing, there is some problem."

[25]

If a company's business grows in a consistent manner over the past years, its stock price is bound to go in an upward direction in that tenure, despite some short-term corrections. And in the same manner, if a company's business deteriorates continuously, its stock price is bound to go in the downward direction irrespective of some short-term appreciations.

It is obvious that an investor would be interested in knowing in an elaborate way the reasons behind a growing business as deteriorating some business is not an achievement, so it doesn't require any special discussion.

Moving ahead, what makes a business grow? The reason behind it lies in the following aspects:

1. Continuous commitment of the company's management to grow the business. This can be clearly evident through rise in the number of sales and profit (Factor no. 1 and 2 of the preliminary screening stage)

2. Efforts of the CFO and management of the company to maximize shareholders' wealth by maintaining a good rate of Return on Equity (Factor no. 3 of the preliminary screening stage)

3. Efforts of the CFO and management of the company to generate returns in an adequate manner over and above the cost of raising funds from borrowing by maintaining a good rate of Return on Capital Employed (Factor no. 4 of the preliminary screening stage)

4. Capability of the management to fund the business growth with the help of borrowing from outside on the basis of strong fundamentals of business without pledging promoter's holdings. This means without pledging promoter's holdings beyond 10% (Factor no. 5 of the preliminary screening)

5. Capability to generate enough wealth and use retained earnings to fund the growth of the business rather than excessive borrowings. This means maintaining Debt to Equity ratio below one. (Factor no. 6 of the preliminary screening)

6. In addition to all the above factors, financials of a great business will also show signs like:

   ➢ CFO/PAT test – at least 75% to 80% of net profits earned in five years are converted into cash

   ➢ Return on Equity is sufficient while maintaining appropriate financial leverage

If all the above factors are satisfied by the company, the share price is bound to go up. But if the price is not going up in a good manner during the last three years even after that, then it is a sign of suspicion as there must be something wrong in the company which is not visible to retail investors and the public at large. Hence, to not go into a dilemma, such stocks are to be avoided in a strict sense. (Factor no. 7 of the preliminary screening)

[26]

"P/E of a stock moves its price up and down – either as a reflection of growth prospects of the business or as a reflection of the temporary effect of sentiments of retail traders."

---

[26]

If the business is not growing in the correct manner as per the factors mentioned for analysis in previous chapters, no need to observe P/E as it is a useless criterion to judge such kind of business in way of value investing. On the other hand, if the business is growing in an adequate manner as per all analytical factors, then P/E is to be observed for valuation analysis as mentioned in the last chapter.

P/E will signal differently in different situations:

1. As the business grows, more and more investors will get attracted to the stock of that company and will move the price up due to constant buying pressure at regular intervals. In that manner, earning per share will grow as a sign of growth in business and price will go up due to continuous attraction by investors into the stock. Observe that both the numerator and denominator of P/E Ratio are increasing and in this way, **P/E will somehow be maintained around that level. In this situation, the Price-Earnings Growth Ratio or PEG as discussed earlier will be maintained at the required level.**

2. When there is growth in business but the price of stock rises more rapidly in comparison to increase in operation levels of business, **P/E will rise above the average level and will indicate overpricing of stock in the general sense. Here, there will be rise in PEG Ratio too.**

3. When there is growth in business but the price of stock is not moving in the same line as compared to that growth, **P/E will fall below the average level and will indicate underpricing of stock in the general sense. Here, there be a decline in PEG Ratio too.**

The common solution to make optimum use of all the three situations as described above is to study the concept of **Average PE of stock or Median PE of stock.** Kindly note that for an initial buying decision, the PEG Ratio will be the deciding factor. Where will the Average PE or Median PE come into play? Let's discuss in the next chapter.

CHAPTER 8

CHOOSING FINAL PLAYERS FOR THE TEAM TO FIGHT WITH INFLATION – PORTFOLIO DESIGNING WITH MULTI-BAGGER POTENTIAL STOCKS

[27]

"Do not put all your eggs in a single basket but also beware that all baskets are not kept in a single big container either. Classification—a tricky but important factor."

[27]

Often it is heard that investment in stocks should be diversified into various stocks for the elimination of risk. The statement is half correct. The fully correct one is that investment in stocks should be diversified among various sectors for managing the risk.

The ideal number of stocks in the portfolio can be anything up to which an investor can keep an eye on a periodic basis i.e. he can keep track of them after investing. Mostly it lies between 10 to 15 stocks. Even many wealth creators like Warren Buffet and Rakesh Jhunjhunwala put a majority of their investment in not more than 8-10 stocks and the same is correct with most value investors.

Now coming to the ideal classification of stocks in which investment is to be done—it is observed that out of the stocks being chosen for investment after the preliminary screening and valuation analysis, an investor should finally select not more than two from any particular sector.

The finalizing of candidates for the initial portfolio should be in the following four steps:

Step 1:

This step will further eliminate stocks which can be given a lesser preference in comparison to others:

1. Give priority to stocks where the combined percentage of shareholdings of promoters and institutional investors in the company has risen as mentioned earlier in this book and delete the ones in which the combined stake has declined by more than 2%. In other words, leave stocks where retail investor holdings rose by more than 2% in that particular quarter.

   Example: Suppose, at the end of December 2019 the shareholdings of the company is 40% by promoters and groups, 40% by institutional investors and 20% by retail investors. But after March 2020, the revised shareholding is 38% by promoters, 38% by institutional investors and 24% by retail investors. Since the combined shareholdings of promoters and institutional investors declined from 80% to 76%, we will put the stock in lesser priority or we can eliminate this from the list. Now just assume a vice versa scenario. Had the combined shareholdings of promoters and institutional investors rose from 76% to 80%, this would have been a good sign in a business where economic moat is already present.

2. Refer to shareholding pattern and leave stocks with the least percentage of promoter's holdings, probably below 35%.

   Note: If the list is not reduced to 20 stocks, then go to the next two sub-steps.

3. Consider Return on Equity of 16 or 17 or 18 in place of original consideration of 15 for final selection. One can do this by applying the filter on the Excel sheet containing the final list

4. Arrange the PEG Ratio from ascending to descending order. Select the ones with up to 1.5 instead of 2.

Even after that if the list is a little above 20 (which usually happens in bearish market), then just keep all of them for further consideration.

Step 2:

From the list shortlisted after step 1, there are two alternatives possible:

1. Invest equally in all the stocks in the list with the total desired investment amount available

2. Evaluate the probability of rise in each stock and as per that finding, take a decision to invest more in the stocks having a higher probability and vice versa

The second one is more useful as this may help increase the overall gain in the future by finding stocks which are not only fundamentally best but are also undervalued in the current scenario and making more investments in them as compared to other potential candidates. This is possible by studying the concept of Average PE or Median PE and using them. This is detailed out in the very next point and the remaining two steps for final stock selection will be discussed on the basis of this finding only.

[28]

"Average or Median PE – the indicator to know how to find out the temporarily undervalued but fundamentally good stocks.

A tiger which stepped back may jump ahead quick and long."

---

[28]

After a list of stocks related to fundamentally sound companies is prepared by taking into account all the steps mentioned till now, you have found investment options which will not result in overall loss of money in the near long term, say one to three years. It may happen with one or two stocks or sectors and investment in them may result in loss because of some negative event occurring in the future related to that company or sector. But this will not probably happen with all the stocks or sectors. Hence, it would be better to diversify the investment amount in various stocks in such a way that can raise the probability to maximize gains along with further mitigation of future risk which may be associated with any particular sector.

Average or Median PE may help identify the tiger that has stepped back temporarily, which means the good stocks which are temporarily undervalued. An investor can use any of them as per his own wish or comfort. I prefer to use both for confirming the output with clarity. The formulae for calculating the Average PE and Median PE are:

1. **Calculation of Average PE Ratio:**

   a. First of all, one needs to take with respect to a stock, its closing price of each month for the last five completed years. The data can be easily obtained from the BSE India website or several other platforms like Money Control. The link to find the same on BSE's site is - https://www.bseindia.com/markets/equity/EQReports/StockPrcHistori.aspx?flag=0

      From this link, one can view and download the data of closing prices related to any stock for any period of time. Download the file and convert the format from CSV to Excel workbook.

b. Keep only the month and closing price column in the file and delete the rest as they are not useful.

c. Against the closing price of each month, just mention the EPS of the year related to that month. Example: In front of 12 cells containing the closing price for all the months of 2014-15, the EPS of FY 2014-15 needs to be mentioned.

d. Divide the price column items by the respective EPS columns.

e. Now you will have 60 PE Ratios for 60 months. Just take the average of all of them in the Excel sheet. This is the **Average PE.**

2. **Calculation of Median PE Ratio:** The steps to calculate Median PE is similar to Average PE Ratio as mentioned above. The only difference is that instead of calculating the average of 60 monthly PE Ratios in step (e) above, one needs to determine the median or say middle value of them in Excel.

My preference – I calculate both for my analysis in the first instance to check. After that, **I often choose Median PE over Average PE** Ratio because while calculating Average PE Ratio, there is a serious limitation. In a case where the price of the share moves unexpectedly in any month in either higher or lower side due to whatever reason, there is a chance that this may impact not only the Monthly PE Ratio of that particular month but also the Average PE Ratio in an unusual manner. But while using Median PE Ratio, there is no such limitation as all the unusually low or high values will automatically shift in the beginning or end, but the median value is the central value which is usually unaffected. One can use anything as per their comfort.

Note: In case some sites provide the median or average PE values, one can use them in the analysis. One of the sites providing such information about every stock is www.screener.in

In case of all the stocks selected after step 2 from the earlier topic, we will follow the next steps as follows:

Step 3:

Just compare the Median PE with the current PE of the stock. If the current PE is approximately equal to or lower than Median PE, then it has a scope of rising in the coming future. But if the current PE of a stock is significantly above the Median PE, then there is a probability that the stock price may fall temporarily in the coming times as this indicates overvaluation up to a certain level. Hence, we need to calculate a ratio called the Current Valuation Coefficient as follows:

Current Valuation Coefficient© = Current PE/Median or Average PE.

It is apparent that the lower the ratio, the better it is. So we need to calculate the ratio of all the stocks in the process of selection after step 2 and arrange the same in ascending order, keeping the stock with more potential gains on top.

Step 4:

As said earlier, we should not select more than two stocks out of one sector for proper diversification. Hence, it is to be checked if there are more than two stocks from a particular sector of business like the chemical industry, automobile industry, information technology, etc. In that case, the two with more favourable Current Valuation Coefficient as calculated in step 3 will be chosen from every sector.

After all these four steps of final selection, now we will have around 5-15 stocks in the final list from various sectors with the best potential to rise in the near future. The only thing to be kept in mind is to just invest more portions comparatively in the stocks whose:

1. Current Valuation Coefficient© is lower

2. Return on Equity is more than 20%

Note: In many cases where companies are fundamentally good and growing continuously, investing in whatever PE generates good results because in growing companies, the price generally moves in the upper direction even with fluctuating PE Ratio. But using Median PE principal helps earn faster on many occasions. It is mainly a comparative tool for adding on dips but is also useful for initial investment on many occasions.

CHAPTER 9

BANKING STOCKS – A DIFFERENT ANIMAL

[29]

"Banking Stocks – Why they demand a different angle of analysis? How to analyze the fundamental characteristics of banking stocks?

Difference in the business model of banking companies as compared to other industries makes it imperative to adopt a different analysis."

---

[29]

Whenever you perform preliminary screening of stocks by using a screener as per the methods mentioned in the books till now, just go to the filter denoting sectors to which stocks in the screen belong and unselect the sector named financial. This is because you need to do the whole process of screening and valuation analysis twice:

- One for all stocks other than banking or financing sector stocks

- Other one for banking sector stocks

Why do we need to do that? This is because banking companies operate in quite a different manner from companies operating other kinds of businesses. As a main component of the operation, they accept deposits from the public and pay interest on that as expense, give loans to the needy and earn interest upon that as income. Banks earn by paying a lower interest on deposits of the public and charge a higher interest on loans given to individuals and business organizations.

Apart from that, banks also make money from other sources like distributing mutual funds, insurance schemes, treasury operations, renting of lockers, etc. Detailed descriptions of businesses and functions of banking companies are of no need here. The only thing relevant for you is to know how the analysis of banking sector stocks is to be done in a different manner.

Analyzing stocks from non-banking sectors requires the use of various concepts and techniques, but analyzing banking stocks is a little tricky in addition to having certain concepts and techniques. But not to worry, as we are here to attempt to discuss all the tricks in a simple manner. As mentioned above, the analysis of banking stocks is different throughout the various stages of stock selection, let's go to those differences one by one in each stage.

1. Preliminary Screening of Banking Stocks

While doing a preliminary screening of banking stocks, five factors out of seven factors will be analyzed in the same manner as done with respect to other stocks. Those five factors are:

- Growth in revenue
- Growth in profit
- Return on Equity and Average Return on Equity
- Pledging of promoter's shares
- Change in price of shares in the last one year and last three years up to the date of analysis

The other two factors are to be given separate considerations namely:

- Debt to Equity ratio
- Return on CE and Average Return on CE

How will these be analyzed in a separate manner? Let's discuss. Banks accept deposits from the public to provide loans to individuals or business organizations. In this way, they accumulate a lot of external debt which will generally be quite more as compared to the net worth or shareholders' fund of banks. We discussed the ideal Debt to Equity ratio as below 1 or 1.5 in the chapter on preliminary screening. But is it possible for banking companies to satisfy this condition? No. Why? For the functioning of banks, it is important to take deposits from the public and this money will be used to grant loans in return. This is essential for operating a banking business. **Hence, the Debt-Equity ratio will not be applicable while analyzing banking sector companies and will not be a factor for preliminary screening of banking stocks.**

Now, let's talk about Return on Capital Employed. Reminding about what this ratio signifies, it denotes the rate at which return is generated by utilizing the total capital employed in business, which means both shareholders' funds and external debt. Restating the above, the debt component in the balance sheet of the bank mainly includes the deposits accepted by banks from the general public on which banks need to pay interest. This amount collected is given as loan to borrowers and for that interest is charged from them. The income of banks in this scenario is the net interest i.e. interest charged by the bank from borrowers minus the interest paid to the public on their deposits. One thing which can be clearly observed is that the bank only acts as a mediator between the two groups of people—one with surplus money and the other one with a shortage of money. By taking money from one group at a comparatively lower rate and providing that amount collected as a loan to another group at a higher rate, banks earn the marginal interest income. Banks have to ultimately bother about the marginal income only.

The deposits received from the public are a liability, but it is not utilized by the bank to perform some activity or build some real assets. Furthermore, the debt will generally remain higher due to the nature of business. Hence, there is no point in calculating DE ratio or including the same in calculating ROCE. The loans granted by the bank to users are assets, but the same is not in the form of some real assets in the company's possession.

Hence, in case of banks, the Return on Capital Employed is not relevant to check upon as the debt component of the bank is not its real borrowing but a liability in the balance sheet against the corresponding asset in the form of loans given to users as a mediator.

So the separate consideration to be given to the Debt to Equity ratio and Return on Capital Employed as stated above means to give no consideration at all to both of these.

2. Valuation Analysis of Banking Stocks

Unlike the factors of preliminary screening, we cannot form the ideal process of valuation analysis with respect to banking stocks by making some changes in the method of valuation with respect to non-banking stocks. Because other than PEG Ratio and Current Valuation Coefficient©, all other aspects of valuation as shown in the chapter on valuation won't be useful in the analysis of banking stocks. Let's discuss the factors useful for doing the same in the case of banking stocks.

After filtering stocks through preliminary screening, just refer to the financial statements of the selected banking company and have a look at the following. This will serve as a general understanding of important concepts of financial statements of a banking company and will be useful for further analysis:

   a. Capital Adequacy Ratio – The Capital Adequacy Ratio (CAR) is a measurement of a bank's available capital expressed as a percentage of a bank's risk-weighted credit exposures. It is also known as capital-to-risk-weighted assets ratio (CRAR). It is used to protect depositors and promote the stability and efficiency of financial systems around the world. There is no need to go into the details of how to calculate as it can be cumbersome for readers with a non-finance background. You will get the ratio figure in financial highlights, management discussion and analysis and notes to consolidate financial statements.

b. Non-Performing Assets details i.e. figures of Gross NPA and Net NPA – Non-Performing Assets means that portion of advances given by the bank and interest earned upon it, which a customer is not able to or willing to pay within the time limit. Lesser the NPA, the better it is for banks. The two ratios to be considered are Gross NPA and Net NPA percentage.

Note: For considering an investment in any banking stock, the information regarding asset quality should be extracted

- By referring to the annual report of the latest year

- Also in the latest quarter result and press release relevant to that quarter. Press release is about the management's comment over various aspects of the company and its performance over the relevant quarter. The press release document along with result for that quarter can be accessed in the investor relation section on the bank's website.

Now, this is the information which is to be extracted from the financial statements, reports, results and press releases of the company. Let us move on to how to gather important analysis from this data:

a. Equity Multiplier or Financial Leverage (EM)

The formula for equity multiplier is the same as in the case of non-banking companies i.e. Total Assets or Total Liabilities divided by Net Worth. We chose the passing criteria for equity multiplier to be lower than 4 or 5 times as the case may be in that respect. But in the case of banking stocks, this criterion is quite low. Because in banking stocks, the loans and advances given to consumers in the ordinary course of banking business will be counted as an asset and in this way, the size of the total assets will be too high as compared to other kinds of businesses. Equity multiplier can be calculated in two ways:

- Either total liability plus net worth/net worth

- Total assets/net worth

The result in both will highlight whether the company is taking excessive deposits and providing excessive loans with respect to its size. In other words, the bank is engaged in more business than it should adhere to with respect to the owner's capital lying in business. Hence, the ideal multiplier for a company in the banking sector has to remain **below 15 times** to ensure that the bank is not crossing the limits in business volume considering its size.

b. Return on Assets (ROA)

Indicates how well the total assets of the banking company are utilized to earn the income for shareholders. The formula is Profit after Tax divided by Total Assets. Higher the ratio, the better it is. For our analysis purpose, we will have the minimum criteria for return on assets as 1% per annum, which means we will consider stocks with return on assets at 1% per annum or more.

Note: Tracing from the above, the combination of

-   equity multiplier i.e. total assets/net worth

-   return on assets i.e. profit after tax/total assets

Result in Return on Equity i.e. profit after tax/net worth.

Hence, after multiplying equity multiplier (ideally below 15) and return on assets (ideally above 1%), the resultant Return on Equity should be 15% or more as referred in the preliminary screening. This will be a proper combination of safety and profitability which results in optimum earnings generation over shareholders' funds or net worth.

c. Capital Adequacy Ratio

RBI sets a minimum percentage at which the capital of a company should stand against its risk-weighted credit exposure. The ratio as required by RBI stands at around 9-10% currently and the bank we are considering shall maintain the capital adequacy ratio at least equal to or more than RBI's minimum requirement. It is good from a safety point of view. Example: HDFC maintained CAR of 17.1% by the end of FY 2018-19 against the minimum requirement of 11.025% by RBI at that point in time. For the same year, Bajaj Finance Limited maintained the capital adequacy ratio at 20.66%. The existing minimum RBI requirement regarding the maintenance of capital adequacy ratio can be found on the RBI website under the section Master Circulars in the document named 'Master Circular - Prudential Norms on Capital Adequacy'. The circular will be separate for urban commercial banks (UCBs) and scheduled commercial bank (SCBs).

d. Gross NPA Ratio

NPA means that proportion of loans and advances given by the bank which the borrower is not able to or willing to return. Out of the percentage and figures of Gross and Net NPA, the Gross NPA is more useful for fundamental analysis of banks.

Often this serves as the most important criteria to judge the banking sector stock. For identifying whether the NPAs of a banking company in the analysis is within manageable limits, one needs to refer to the website of RBI i.e. rbi.org.in. On this website, RBI makes available the financial stability reports which are issued at six-month intervals i.e. June and December, and its annual report which is issued annually. These reports will contain information about the Gross NPA ratios of scheduled commercial banks (SCBs) in total. Example: The financial stability report dated 27 December 2019 stated the SCBs' Gross NPA ratio as 9.3%.

Hence, for our analysis of a banking company, we should compare two figures:

- the general percentage of Gross NPA for SCBs as mentioned by RBI in its latest financial stability report or annual report

- the Gross NPA ratio of a banking company in its latest reported results

The banking company which we are analyzing should have a Gross NPA ratio at least 20% lesser than the general ratio for SCBs as mentioned by RBI in its reports.

Example: The Gross NPA ratio of HDFC Bank Ltd as per its results for the quarter which ended on December 2019 was at 1.42% in comparison to that of 9.3% in RBI's released financial stability report for the half-year ending December 2019. So it passes the criteria as 20% below 9.3% GNPA in general is 7.4%. But HDFC Bank's ratio is 1.42%, which is quite low and manageable. For FY 2018-19, Bajaj Finance Ltd had a Gross NPA ratio at 1.54% which is favourable too.

e. Provisioning Coverage Ratio

Provisioning Coverage Ratio (PCR) refers to the prescribed percentage of funds set aside by banks for covering prospective losses due to bad loans. If a company attains growth in its revenue, profits and EPS by maintaining a high provisioning ratio of say 65% or more, then it is quite a good indication. Higher the provisioning coverage ratio, the better it is. Though the provisioning results in lowering of profits in the current period, it cleans the balance sheet by providing adequate funds to meet any NPAs in the future by directly writing off with the amount set aside as PCR in the preceding years instead of hitting the profit and loss account. Hence, in a year, when the banking company earns more profits, it should provide greater provisioning coverage ratio for avoiding any fall in reported profits in the future.

Like Gross NPA ratio, RBI publishes the SCB's provisioning coverage ratio in general too. Hence, here also, while considering a banking company stock, one needs to compare the provisioning coverage ratio of a banking company with the ratio published by RBI. Example: In financial stability report for the half-year ending on December 2019, the provisioning coverage ratio for SCBs was mentioned by RBI as 61.5%, whereas in the annual report related to the last completed year of HDFC Bank i.e. in FY 2018-19, the provisioning coverage ratio stood at 71.36% which was quite satisfactory and substantially high as compared to RBI's average figure.

However, if a company's PCR stands above 65%, then it is good no matter the average PCR as identified by RBI as its report is a higher figure.

f. Net Interest Margin

Net interest margin means the excess interest earned on advances over interest paid on deposits taken from the public divided by the average amount of advances given by the bank.

$$NIM = \frac{(\text{Interest earned} - \text{Interest expense}) * 100}{\text{Average Advances}}$$

It is apparent that higher the NIM, the better it is. The higher rate of NIM indicates a healthy earning model in the company, but it is rumoured that excessive NIM increases the future probability of occurrence of higher NPAs. This is because concentration to increase NIM will result in higher loan advancing by the bank, which will increase the chance of future NPAs. This interpretation doesn't always hold correct and may result in loss of multi-bagger potential stocks a number of times. In my opinion, it is a profitability measure ratio and should not be mixed up with safety concerns just by referring to the NIM percentage. If the banking company is able to maintain other factors namely:

- equity multiplier below 15

- ROE above 15%

- ROA above 1%

- capital adequacy ratio above the minimum RBI requirement

- controlled Gross NPA ratio

- adequate provisioning coverage ratio

Then the NIM margin will automatically be appropriate as per the company's operations. So just keep the concept of NIM in mind but do not make any criteria for that. We need to make our analysis process simple and not get ourselves confused with too many criteria.

g. PEG Ratio and Current Valuation Coefficient©

The concept of PEG Ratio is to be applied in the same manner as discussed in the previous parts of the book and the qualifying limit will also be the same in the case of banking stock——it's better if it is below one and acceptable if below 2.

Furthermore, the concept of Current Valuation Coefficient© will also be the same for banking stocks and non-banking stocks. As explained earlier, this exercise is adopted mainly for add on dips and also for prioritization of stocks in case of fresh investment. In this, the position of PE Ratio is to be considered in connection with the Median PE of the last five years.

h. Shareholding Pattern

Shareholding analysis will not be different in the case of banking business as promoters and institutional investors will also react to potential banking stocks in the same way they do for potential non-banking stocks.

After all these steps, it can be said that the banking company stock which adheres to the principles mentioned in this chapter can be taken as the prospective buying candidate for our selection.

Note: Please make a habit to read the press releases given by banks for the purpose of providing various information for investors and other users. Normally, the press release is given along with quarterly results published by the company. There remains a very important section in that press release called 'Asset quality measures'. This section can also be referred to in either the annual report of the last completed year or the latest announced results of the banking company.

In the press release, the bank provides NPAs, capital adequacy and other required information. It is good practice to refer to the latest quarter press release before taking a decision to purchase. But while reading, just be cautious about any information which is presented in an exaggerated form, which means overstating any factors for marketing purposes. Reading press releases along with financial results is a good practice.

SECTION - 3

POST ACQUISITION
ANALYSIS AND SALE

THE BAD THING IS THAT TIME FLIES; THE GOOD THING IS THAT YOU ARE THE PILOT – OBSERVING WHETHER INVESTMENTS PERFORM AS INTENDED

[30]

"Review of the latest events is a necessary step to ensure that the stocks bought are performing as intended.

There is one good thing and bad thing about time—it changes. Be alert to unfavourable changes."

[30]

Yes Bank's share – the stock which turned a nightmare for investors. A stellar performer with around 43 times the returns since its listing in 2005 to September 2018, and it was a fundamentally strong candidate till then too.

But then, suddenly that YES turned into a NO. The stock fell down by around 30% in one day following a news article. The news was that the asset quality divergence in the case of Yes Bank stood at more than 300%, whereas for its peers like Axis Bank, SBI and Bank of India, it was merely around 25%. In other words, the quantum of NPA (Non-Performing Assets) as discovered by the central bank in Yes Bank was more than three times extra i.e. four times than what it was actually disclosing in its books. It was disclosing in its books NPAs of around Rs 2,000 crore whereas the actual figure, as ought to be believed by RBI, was beyond Rs 8,000 crore. This amounted to the NPA ratio out of advances given by the bank at the rate of 3%. This figure was considered to be quite significant upon viewing it as a percentage of revenue or profits of Yes Bank for the Financial Year 2018-19. The market was quick to assess the situation and after an extreme selling pressure, the stock turned down and the story till now is known to all.

This is not a comment or judgement from me regarding the future prospects of Yes Bank but is just an example as to how investors should remain conscious while holding their investments in the market to enable a timely exit.

Time changes and with time we need to change our actions sometimes. We should not be affected by short-term movements in our investments but only when those movements are not a sign of change in the bright future of the company or sector. Because in that scenario, we need to be cautious enough to interpret such information and act accordingly.

Another example is Zee Entertainment Enterprises Ltd. It was a great business as the stock price rose from 250 in 2014 to 580 in 2018. But the pledged holdings of promoters rose to 96% and this began to rise from 2018. The result was that the stock price went from 570 to 140 within two years. This is just the reverse of what we expect to earn i.e. 570 to 140 instead of 140 to 570.

A similar case happened with Jyothy Labs Ltd. Its stock price rose from 85 in 2014 to 245 in 2018. But increase in pledged holdings of promoters over the period plus deteriorating quarter to quarter results brought the stock price from 245 in 2018 to 115 in 2020.

The first indication of any such information will be clearly evident in the stock price because of the iron-magnet relationship. So an investor must be attentive to information about the companies in which he has invested. This will enable him to exit timely if the information is so vital that it may affect the company's future prospects.

The only remedy to not suffer due to this is to continuously monitor the news and stock price actions in a company. See, it is quite normal for the price of a stock to move up and down by around 20-25% in normal life without any reason. But one should also accept the fact that a good company this year cannot necessarily be good in the coming years. In case any such negative things occur with your investment in any stock, you can still dispose your holdings in such shares and come out with a reduced profit or minimal loss, as the case may be.

Being awake to all the changes is a possible way to overcome timely. No worries.

[31]

"Yearly, Quarterly, Weekly and Ad-hoc analysis and actions is a must to avoid losing money over one stock.

Remaining invested and observing business as a sleeping partner with an option to come out upon finding something odd is a good power in hand."

---

[31]

Ad-hoc – After buying a stock, you need to be awake to any odd news or event or finding which can deteriorate the earnings of the company or its credibility in the near future. With many types of stocks and various parameters of growth across many industries, such types of awakening news can come in many ways. One needs to be cautious enough to trace those events timely and evaluate its possible impact on the company's future growth and survival. Generally, the news can come to an investor in two ways:

1. If the investor is keen to see the news of a company or industry daily on mediums such as moneycontrol.com, economic times etc., he can meet with such information

2. A more obvious one—the price of a stock will suddenly start falling in huge percentage either in a day or couple of days. Example: Yes Bank's share fell down by around 25% within a day of the news regarding asset quality divergence.

If any such drop occurs in the price suddenly, one needs to dig dipper to know why this happened and evaluate as per the situation.

3. Such news can also be sector-wise. This type of situation generally occurs when there is no company-wise issue but some serious new issues arising within a sector. Example: Pharmacy sector after 2017 in India.

In such a scenario, an investor needs to act promptly and come out as soon as possible from the holdings.

A practical way to track this kind of possibility is to just have a look at your portfolio once daily after the morning session, around 12 PM every day. If there is any stock with a decline in price by more than 10% within that day, then look upon the news and announcement section regarding that stock on BSE and any other online platform to confirm the same. If the news seems like a sign of any future threat, just analyze the news fully and make a timely exit. If there is no such news available, then keep your holdings intact as this may be a temporary fall due to market sentiments. Not to worry.

Weekly – Whether or not there is any company or sector-specific news, or even if there is no unexpected drop in price, an investor should never omit to refer the news section for a particular stock on some good platforms and in fact multiple platforms simultaneously like moneycontrol.com, BSE or NSE websites and any other suitable way.

Attention is to be given to any possible change in the shareholding patterns of the company, changes in the main line of the company's businesses and government permissions or notifications regarding a particular company or sector.

Special attention is to be given to stocks which have moved down by around 25% or more from the last highest price without any nation-wide recession during that period.

Quarterly or Annually – Purchase of fundamentally good stocks depends only and only on the growth prospects of a company which is evident not only through past results while analyzing but also in the future results declared anytime by the company. Hence, after the declaration of every quarter's results by the company, the following procedure is to be performed:

1. New list of multi-bagger stocks is to be prepared after applying all the factors of preliminary screening and valuation analysis

2. Ensure that all the shares which are already held on the basis of previous list(s) are covered in the new list prepared

3. In case any stock which was already held is not available in the new list prepared after the current quarter, identify why that stock is not in the new list. Identify which parameter is lacking and avoid it from being considered as multi-bagger in the future. Note that the assessment to be made involves whether signs of economic moat are still present and not regarding valuation at that moment. If the company is growing quarter to quarter but the stock is slightly overvalued then there is nothing to worry about. But if the situation governs that the business of a company is not going to rise in terms of revenue or profits, or if any other factor of economic moat is deteriorating, then it is better to make a timely escape from the holdings of that share and invest in new ones

This is because the reason for which you were holding it is now not available with that stock. This may happen with one or two shares at a time out of the whole portfolio and it's acceptable because you will get an opportunity to exit timely without losing a major amount. This will also help keep the portfolio returns at the desired level on an overall basis because you are eliminating losers timely and maintaining winners in the team.

CHAPTER 11

WATER THE FLOURISHING PLANTS AND NOT THE DEAD ONES – ADD ON DIPS VERY CAREFULLY

[32]

"In companies with businesses having economic moat, either continuous growth in EPS along with PEG Ratio below two or fall in current PE to get closer or slightly lower than Median PE are the only two bases to add on dips. Every fall in stock price is not a buying opportunity unless the business growth in the coming future seems certain.

Every step back is not a tiger's move."

[32]

If the growth in business has reached a saturation level, then there is no point in doing PE analysis. If the business does not grow or if any fundamental aspect gets off track, then what will you do with the valuation? It's useless.

Hence, only fundamentally good stocks which satisfy all the parameters to be called as multi-bagger potential stocks provide a good opportunity to add on dips when:

1. There is continuous growth in EPS on year to year and quarter to corresponding quarter of the preceding year

2. The PEG Ratio is maintained below 2

3. The PE of a stock falls down to a value surrounding the Median PE or lower than the Median PE

It is quite surprising that in the near future, a stock can be available at a higher price but a lower PE. This means the stock is cheaper even if available at a higher price. Example: In just recent times, GMM PFaudler stock was available at Rs 1,184 on 20 May 2019 and at that time, the PE Ratio was 44. After two weeks i.e. on 4 June 2019, the stock price was Rs 1,260 but the PE Ratio was 36. Here, the stock was available at a higher price but the PE Ratio was lower which dictates a very surprising thing that the stock was cheaper at Rs 1,260 than what it was at Rs 1,184.

This is similar to a situation where a plot of land was available at around Rs 1 lakh in an area and the prediction was that in the next five years, the expected future price of the same plot would be Rs 3 lakh. This means a potential of 200% gain in the next five years.

After a passage of three months, suppose a government project got approved near that plot which made the price of land rise in that area. Now the same plot is available at

Rs 1.5 lakh, and the future expected price also increased to Rs 6 lakh. Now the earning potential rose to 300%.

The irony is that the plot is available at a higher price i.e. Rs 1.5 lakh in place of Rs 1 lakh, which was prior to the government's project approval. But the earning potential rose from 200% to 300%. So effectively the land price is cheaper at Rs 1.5 lakh than what it was at Rs 1 lakh.

Hence, in stock analysis also, the future growth potential of stock price depends upon the PE at the moment and not stock price. Why? The answer is PE Ratio means the current price of the stock divided by the latest EPS. When EPS rises year to year or quarter to quarter, the price will also rise accordingly, sooner or later.

Sometimes, the stock price rises faster than the corresponding increase in EPS which results in higher PE Ratio. This signifies that the stock is overvalued or expensive for that moment as compared to previous situations.

Also, sometimes it happens that the stock price rises but at a lower rate than the rise in EPS, which ultimately lowers the PE. This signifies that the stock is comparatively cheaper or undervalued than that in the previous situation, even though it is available at a higher price. **This type of situation is perfect for adding on dips if PEG Ratio supports at that moment i.e. if it's below 1.5.**

Apart from this, the daily up or down movement in the price of a stock, belonging to sentiments of traders in the stock market, also puts the PE Ratio of that stock at comparatively higher or lower values respectively on a temporary basis. This also gives an opportunity to add on dips.

Hence, the crux is that lowering of PE due to

- **either slow rise in the stock price in wake of increasing EPS of the company**

- **temporary fall in stock price due to normal buying and selling of traders in the stock market**

opens the door for constructive adding on dips. This is even more beneficial when the PE reaches near Median PE or lower than that, provided the growth in fundamental terms is on its track.

Note: Whenever the PE Ratio of any stock is at the highest or lowest value in the last five years, then it requires a serious relook at all the fundamental analysis factors associated with that stock before taking an investment decision. Well, it is not an item of worry because by calculating Current Valuation Coefficient© during valuation stage of analysis, these kinds of stocks will always be in the bottom of the list and are easy to avoid in the final decision-making.

Some people may have a doubt whether a PE analysis is actually needed to be undertaken for adding on dips. Because in a situation where a company is fundamentally strong enough and is growing continuously, then its stock price will automatically move in the upward direction over a considerably longer period of time. So isn't it good while buying at any PE Ratio till the time the company is on the growth track and the PEG Ratio is below 2?

The answer to this is it is absolutely acceptable to purchase fundamentally good stock at whatever PE when the target is long-term buying. But it also holds true that if a stock is purchased occasionally at a lower PE, then it will provide a good chance of booking higher profits in the future by maintaining a lower average purchase rate. This is because it will rise quickly to bring a rise in price in sync with the rise in EPS of the company and signifies just a momentum change.

[33]

"It doesn't matter at what price you buy; what matters is the earning potential the investment has beyond that point.

Stock Price in Rupee Terms – Is it really important?"

---

[33]

Situation 1:

One stock is available at Rs 5,000 per share and another one at Rs 100 per share. Many choose the second one thinking that by spending Rs 5,000, he can buy 50 shares of that company while he can only get one share in the first one within the budget of Rs 5,000. This principle is often applied by investors in the following manner:

- Choosing random penny stock – Some traders or investors just get attracted to stocks like Sundaram Multi Pap, Web-sol Energy, Achal investment and many such penny stocks just because they are available within the range of Rs 10. However, using Rs 10,000 what is the use of buying more than 1000 shares of such a company? Without analyzing the fundamentals of the company and linking the status of its price with its growth in terms of PEG Ratio, how can one blindly put his money in such stocks just to buy a huge number of stocks with a limited investment amount? Instead of this, investing in one fundamentally good stock at the price of Rs 10,000 is far more useful. The price at which one buys a stock doesn't matter. The only thing which matters is the future probable returns associated with it.

- Choosing a stock after due fundamental analysis, but giving preference to Rs 100 stock rather than Rs 1,000 – See, prioritizing stocks within the list of potential multi-bagger stocks will only depend upon the PEG Ratio, Current Valuation Coefficient© and favourable changes in shareholding patterns in terms of the combined holding of promoters and institutional investors. This means just a stock at Rs 100 will not prove that it will rise faster than Rs 1000 stock. This is an incorrect notion. Here too, what matters is the future probable returns associated with it.

Situation 2:

Two stocks were bought – both at Rs 100 per share. The price of the first one reached from Rs 100 to Rs 160 while the price of the other reached from Rs 100 to Rs 40.

Which should you buy more in order to add on dips?

The answer is that full multi-bagger potential analysis is to be done not only after each quarter result but also while making any purchase decision—initial or add on dips.

Applying the iron-magnet combo effect into the price of a stock, it is understood that as far as the company grows, the price of the stock tends to move in the upward direction in the long run. So while applying add on dips in a stock that moved from Rs 100 to Rs 160, the decision will be made only on the availability of the following:

- Multi-bagger potential i.e. preliminary screening plus valuation analysis

- Better Current Valuation Coefficient© i.e. near to 1 or a little lower than that

Also, as stated in the earlier topic, the stock may be at Rs 160 instead of Rs 100 but then its valuation may also be cheaper than that was when its price stood at Rs 100.

A stock rising from Rs 100 to Rs 160 will have such potential to provide multi-bagger returns in the future due to probable continuous growth in the future. But do you think that such potential to provide multi-bagger returns can be available in a stock which has fallen from Rs 100 to Rs 40? It is true that traders' sentiments often make the price fall in the short-term but not so significantly.

It's not wrong to consider the fall in stock price for adding on dips but the only thing to be kept in mind is that the decision should be based on the combination of multi-bagger and Current Valuation Coefficient© tests.

[34]

"Stock getting out of the fundamental track or need of money to meet some objectives in the near future are the only ideal reasons to sell a stock.

Before selling out a stock, just consider why you bought it."

---

[34]

Situation 1 – Financial Need:

It is good to sell off some portion of the portfolio and keep the amount aside in a savings account or short-term fixed deposit to meet the near future objective. Just as the priority of buying is decided on the basis of lower Current Valuation Coefficient©, priority will be given for selling out to that stock which has the highest Current

Valuation Coefficient©. It means that out of all the fundamentally good stocks held in the portfolio, the one with the most expensive valuation will be sold out first and so on.

Situation 2 – Losing Fundamental Values:

Whether there is any financial need or not, if a stock gets out of the fundamental track at any moment, we just need to sell it off. How to judge if a stock gets out of track? The answer is discontinuation by the company to fulfil any of the fundamental parameters as follows:

1. No further rise in revenue, profit before tax or EPS

2. Pledging of promoter's holdings rises beyond 10%

3. Debt to Equity ratio rises above 1 or 1.5 as considered by investors (Applicable except in banking companies)

4. Financial leverage element in ROE rises above 4 or 5 as the case may be

5. Falling ROE and ROCE below the minimum threshold

6. Cash generation has become slower, which means deteriorating CFO/PAT ratio

7. PE Ratio has reached a very high level as compared to the average of the past five or three years

Other than these reasons, never ever sell a stock just because it already provided a return of 10%, 20%, 50%, 100% or even 500%. Also, it is needless to mention that a stock is not to be sold out only because there is a temporary fall in stock price or the stock price is not moving up significantly just after buying. Sell only in the above-mentioned situations.

SECTION - 4

DON'T FOLLOW THE LOSER'S PATH AND DO WHAT WINNERS DO

CHAPTER 12

KNOW WHAT LOSERS IN THE STOCK MARKET DO TO AVOID THEIR DEEDS IN YOUR LIFE

[35]

"How can one succeed in the stock market if he is more careful about buying fruits and vegetables than of buying stocks?

Try to learn from others' mistakes; you won't live enough to try them all in your life span."

[35]

Most readers will feel while reading this chapter that I am counting their mistakes and presenting them here. But it's ok. Face the truth or wait till it turns into a fierce battlefield.

Acknowledging general mistakes made by losers in the share market may help you recognize if you are a silent victim of these habits and whether they prove to be a great hurdle in your way of wealth creation. You need to know them just to avoid repetition in the future. The mistakes generally opted by retail investors in the market along with their solutions are as follows:

1. **Investing only on the basis of low PE and PB ratio**

   The PE Ratio is not useful in isolation. Its linkage with the Growth Ratio of the company and Average PE Ratio of the last five years is the criteria to consider an investment opportunity, provided all other multi-bagger factors are present in the company.

   Simply buying a company's stock because it is available at a cheaper rate is of no use. **It's acceptable to buy a wonderful company at a fair price but not a fair company at a wonderful price.**

2. **Not able to purchase more quantities i.e. add on dips at higher prices in the future**

   The growing business of a company and the rising price of the stock is just an iron-magnet combo. If the business of a company grows more and more year after year or quarter after quarter, its stock price will also move in an upward direction continuously. You purchased a share today at say Rs 100 because at this moment:

   - the business of the company has economic moat (preliminary screening is satisfactory)

   - the valuation of stock is not expensive at the price of Rs 100 (valuation analysis is satisfactory)

   - the shareholding pattern changes are not against the flow

   After one or more quarter or suppose after a year, if the stock is running at Rs 150, what should an investor consider? He should only consider whether the economic moat is still present in the company's business which evidences future probable growth of the business, whether the valuation of stock (Current Valuation Coefficient©) is reasonable with the current scenario at the price of Rs 150 and the shareholding pattern changes are not in a negative direction. That's it.

But in place of this, what he considers is that he bought it at Rs 100 per share just three months ago. Now a little more is needed to purchase at Rs 150, so it is expensive. He then decides not to buy at that price.

He will simply miss the chance as he ignores the iron-magnet combo inherent in the rise in business and rise in its share price. The stock price may rise in the next one or two years to Rs 200, 250, 300 or even more because the stock may have more potential now. He will see this like a mute spectator. Utter foolishness.

Don't hesitate to buy great stocks repeatedly with increasing prices to earn the maximum in the long run with that stock. Even when the stock is at 52 weeks high or a lifetime high or even if they have already provided multi-bagger returns in the near past, its price can rise further if the multi-bagger analysis is still supportive.

Rakesh Jhunjhunwala might have purchased Titan at Rs 40, Rs 80 and Rs 400 and maybe even later. The stock price didn't go back and was in the range of Rs 1200 at the beginning of 2020. This is because every time he bought the stock, he was sure of the presence of economic moat and the reasonableness of the price at the time he made fresh investments in it. In recent phases, I continuously bought stocks like Alkyl Amine Chemical Ltd, Asian Paints and GMM PFaudler (recent) at various prices over a period of two or more years.

3. **Not saying bye-bye to a stock at the correct time**

   Stocks should be sold if the reason for which it was bought doesn't sustain any more. The reason may include:

   - Arrival of some news which will probably result in revenue and EPS going down in the coming quarter or shortly thereafter. The news will be strong enough to show correction in the market price of share suddenly. Investors should play cautiously in such a situation and exit immediately. Example of Yes Bank as discussed earlier

   - EPS of the company reaching break-even stage i.e. not rising further

   - Company's entry into a new business in a substantial manner and such new business is not at all related in any way for existing operations

   - And many other such indications of the stock losing its fundamental strength. This can be quite easy to trace if a person regularly analyzes the quarterly result, ad-hoc referring of news in case of a sudden crash in stock price, abnormal selling of holdings by promoters and institutional investors, etc.

Alternatively, the stock can be sold when another investment opportunity with more satisfying factors of analysis comes into play. Multi-bagger analysis is to be done at various moments like slowdown of the economy and quarterly scheduled analysis post quarterly results announcement by the company. Each time the analysis is done, a fresh list will be generated. In that fresh list, the stocks which came in the earlier multi-bagger analysis will mostly be repeated, but the list will also contain new stocks which have become more potential opportunities in current times in comparison to some of the stocks in the earlier list. In this scenario, it's better to switch when the more satisfying factors lie with a new company.

Also, there may be a situation that the stocks which were in the old list did not gain a place in the new list. In such a case, an investor should analyze immediately whether the missing companies have suffered in any factor owing to their fundamental strength due to which they didn't gain any place in the new list. If there is any such issue, it's better to exit timely without profit or with limited loss and invest in some other good company.

Hence, as soon as the reason on the basis of which the investment was made loses its character, exit the stock without a second thought. And in the book, the basis of selection is the fundamental strength and reasonable valuation along with favourable shareholding pattern activities. So, as soon as there is negative change evident in any of these things, just exit.

If a stock is losing its character of growth, do not assume that there will be some turnaround in the company in the near future without any solid reason. No need to get stuck in that company and miss other opportunities. If the food on your plate is good and as per your wish, then what is the need to run after something else?

After selling do not look back at that stock to see whether its price is still increasing. You purchased for a reason. You sold because that reason expired. That's it.

4. **Knowing the deterioration of fundamentals, but still holding stocks to recover the loss incurred**

    Suppose after buying a stock purely on the basis of fundamental strength, you suddenly notice any of the following occurrences:

    -   Revenue and profit start falling in the next quarter as compared to the same quarter in the previous year by 10% or more

    -   The promoters sell 10% stake in the open market

- The company raises debt portion in its capital structure and the total Debt-Equity ratio rises to 2:1

- Sudden news in the market which makes it sure that either revenue or profits of the business will fall in the near future

And as a result, if the stock price starts falling down, then the stock is to be sold immediately. Immediate selling is to be opted irrespective of the price at the current moment because if things keep deteriorating with respect to the company's business, the price of the stock will also keep falling. If you do not accept minimum or limited loss, then your loss can multiply in the future. You just have to come out by bearing even 50% loss to save at least that amount for future use to invest in good stock.

Example: Tata Coffee Ltd—steep fall in stock price owing to a decline in its profit and EPS during FY 2017-18. Suzlon Energy Ltd—the journey of declining share price from Rs 420 in 2008 to Rs 3 in 2020. Just search for any company with an overall fall in its stock price in the last three to five years. The reason will be common—deterioration in factors evident of economic moat (preliminary screening). Also, these kinds of experiences are quite common in PSU units like

- Steel Authority of India Ltd where the stock price was at Rs 53 in 2019 from its lifetime high of Rs 280 in 2008 and it is further deteriorating.

- Another PSU unit example is BHEL, where its lifetime high stands at around Rs 360 and the present price is Rs 50 and further declining.

Just avoid these kinds of losing players in your portfolio and even if you include them by mistake, just exit at the time they begin showing their true colours. See, all parameters of growth, valuation and final selection as stated in the section 'Hunt for Multi-Bagger Stocks' are to be fulfilled in combination and not isolation, for only then a stock can be called as having multi-bagger potential.

It's as simple as that; just exit as soon as possible upon the first sign of slowdown if the reason for purchasing stock was the growth prospects.

I know emotions won't allow you to accept the loss and come out; they will only tell you to wait for some kind of recovery or bounce back. This is the most common problem, but you need to kill your thoughts, exit the losers immediately and invest the sale amount in winners. Winners may take a little time but will soon recover the loss caused by losers. Just trust and invest in them.

Don't lose money – This is the first principle of investing in stock.

5. **Tendency to book short profits and avoid bigger pleasures waiting ahead**

Pleasant lies – Wow! Harsh truths – Oh No!

This is the character and sarcastic reaction of about 90% people in their lifestyle to these two types of results or situations in every walk of life. The stock market is no different.

Suppose an investor buys two stocks, A Ltd and B Ltd. One unit of both was purchased at Rs 100 each. After one month, A Ltd's stock price reaches Rs 140 while the price of B Ltd's stock went down to Rs 60. What will be the obvious reaction of the investor regarding both the stocks?

- For A Ltd – Wow, the price has reached Rs 140. Let me sell it immediately and book profit before it comes down. I will purchase it again when the price comes down temporarily.

- For B Ltd – Oh no, the price has fallen to Rs 60. Let's wait for the future. When it reaches Rs 100 or more, I will sell it then. And the price is too good to buy more. Let's purchase one more share at Rs 60. Then I will have the cost of Rs 80 per share in hand. When the price regains to Rs 100, I will have huge profits by selling them.

Instead of doing this, he should relook the fundamentals status of both the companies. There is quite a definite chance that applying the multi-bagger test again will prove that he should hold A Ltd stock as it will generate more gains ahead and it can with great possibility suggest that B Ltd stock has to be sold immediately at Rs 60 because it may fall beyond limits in the future because the fundamentals may have started deteriorating from thereon.

It is told earlier that if a stock is chosen through the multi-bagger test, then it is to be sold in the future when the test starts getting proven wrong from any particular moment, no matter if it is at profit or loss in the current situation.

Do not maintain the common strategy blindly followed by many investors of selling stocks in profit and holding or adding on dips for those in loss. This is one of the reasons why 80% of people lose money ultimately in the stock market.

Also, **if a stock continues to be a promising candidate to give multi-bagger returns in the future too, then do not sell it to buy again at a lower level in the future**. Just keep holding the current investment in that stock and if it comes down, then add on dips on the basis of Current Valuation Coefficient© and PEG Ratio as mentioned in the earlier parts of the book.

6. **Adding on dips in shares where prices fall without checking the condition of the fundamental strengths**

As clearly mentioned in the chapter related to principles of adding on dips, an investor should accumulate more units of a stock only when the factors of preliminary screening, valuation analysis and shareholding changes are in favour of purchasing at that moment. Merely adding on dips on the basis of fall in the price of a stock is quite foolish and an expensive mistake. You can never imagine where the fall will end because there is no limit to which the price of a stock can fall if the business of a company is deteriorating. Just hate the temptations surrounding you which say "Listen, A Ltd stock was at Rs 150. Now it is available at Rs 60. Just buy it." Stop listening to all these idiotic things.

7. **Purchasing because some big investor or institutional investor invested or promoters increased the stake**

In an earlier part of the book, the above-mentioned signs are stated as positive but do remember that these can be a positive sign only when the stock passes the multi-bagger test. The data alone does not have any great significance if the analysis does not support that stock to be treated as a multi-bagger candidate.

You may purchase imitating the actions of the types of big players as mentioned above, but in the future, there may be a case where you don't get timely information of their exit from that stock. And this may cause a delay in selling at your end and may lead to a loss.

Just apply the principles mentioned in the book and maintain a portfolio as per that. Don't opt for any shortcuts by blindly imitating others whether he is your neighbour or a classy investor like Rakesh Jhunjhunwala. If you still want to try your fortune in the stocks chosen by them, just conduct a multi-bagger test on those particular stocks and take a decision only on the basis of satisfying results.

8. **Taking the negative experience in stock investing as a personal failure**

Changes occurring in the fundamental factors related to a company are not within the reach of any retail investor. So if you are bound by the law of fundamental testing, you need to buy when the fundamentals are in place and indicate a good future for the company. But at the same time, you need to sell when there is any sign of deterioration in the fundamental strength of the company. Out of the 10 companies selected for creating a portfolio, as per the fundamental testing, it may be evident after the passage of a little time that one or two stocks out of the portfolio lose fundamental factors and such deterioration can be of any type as stated in the book so far. This situation only suggests selling that stock and keeping the money to invest in the best among others. This is a rule or oath. Just because your estimate proves wrong in the case of one or two companies doesn't mean you need to lose trust in yourself or the credibility of the other good stocks in your portfolio. There is always a chance that one or two companies out of the team selected by you, as per the multi-bagger testing, may prove to be wrong, but this will never impact the overall returns of your portfolio as others will not leave the character of multi-bagger. Just remember, "Door of peace and happiness is only opened with the key of trust." Keep selecting 10-15 stocks as per the fundamental analysis. Regularly eliminate one or two which do not prove good ahead by immediately selling and keep the money handy to invest in better opportunities ahead. This is a lifetime cycle to be followed. Just refer to the example below.

Suppose you invested in eight companies finalized by you as per the fundamental analysis and you invest equal proportion in them:

Stock Name	Invested Amount
A Ltd	1000
B Ltd	1000
C Ltd	1000
D Ltd	1000
E Ltd	1000
F Ltd	1000
G Ltd	1000
H Ltd	1000

Now suppose after six months, the value of the investment in stocks reaches as follows:

Stock Name	Invested Amount	Current Value	Profit/ Loss
A Ltd	1000	2100	1100
B Ltd	1000	1600	600
C Ltd	1000	1400	400
D Ltd	1000	1250	250
E Ltd	1000	1100	100
F Ltd	1000	1090	90
G Ltd	1000	1210	110
H Ltd	1000	890	(110)
Total	**8000**	**10640**	**2640**

As it is clearly apparent, the overall portfolio stands at a profit of Rs 2640 over the invested amount of Rs 8000. In case of the stock in loss i.e. H Ltd, if you find out that the fundamentals are degrading in their value, then you must exit immediately bearing a limited loss of Rs 110 to avoid any harm to the profit generated by the other good stocks in the coming future. In fact, the same treatment is to be given to the stocks in profit too. Suppose G Ltd stock is in profit but the decline in EPS has started from a high in the corresponding quarter last year, then you need to come out timely because there may be a case that the declining EPS may cause the stock price to fall further in the coming days or weeks. Just exit when the future probability is affected. And after exiting, never look back at the price of these stocks until and unless they automatically come in the list of multi-bagger tested stocks in the future.

Invest in stocks with the best probability of rising through the multi-bagger test but do not prove your loyalty to it by holding even when the fundamentals begin deteriorating in the future or near future. The selling and coming out, in this case, won't be a case of personal failure but a sign of obtaining maturity in real terms.

9. **Selling winner stocks because of a temporary fall in stock price or no significant rise for a few months**

   For a value investor, investing in stocks is just like having partial ownership in a business and nothing else. Just watching the share price again and again and getting affected by the short-term fall will not lead you far from the losers in the market. With regard to your holdings, you need to do periodic reviews as follows:

   1. Ad-hoc checking of news sections related to that particular stock in case some important notification comes. This is to ensure whether it has some impact on the price of share or fundamentals of the company in the present or near future

   2. Weekly review of news sections and announcements of the company to gather indications about change in the line of business, unfavourable impact on the business or any other important news

3. Quarterly review of the stock to ensure that the new financial reporting in the underlying business is on track in terms of preliminary screening, valuation analysis factors and changes in shareholding patterns

If the fundamentals of a company, along with shareholding patterns, prove that it is still on the growth track, just hold the stock no matter what the current market price of the share is. Buying and selling forces conflict in the stock market and the price of any stock may move in either direction in the short-run, but if the company's management is able to maintain growth in its business on a continuous basis, the stock price is bound to rise in the long run.

Fundamentals of a company are long-term drivers of the stock price while the sentiments of buyers and sellers of stock in the market prove to be the short-term drivers. If you purchased a stock trusting the long-term drivers of the stock price, then do not sell on the basis of short-term drivers. The company's intact fundamentals will make the share price bounce back in the long run and give returns bound to be in the company's stock with respect to its growth.

Long-term growth in the share price of fundamentally good companies does not depend on market movement as a whole i.e. Sensex and Nifty positions. It depends only on the fundamentals of that company and nothing else. Sometimes, a major crash in the economy or world economies like that at the time of COVID-19 recently can bring the price of almost all stocks down by a significant rate. But good companies survive the attack of any situation over the long run. **It is quite possible for a good company to generate positive returns even in a bearish market.**

CHAPTER 13

REQUIREMENTS, HABITS, EXPERIENCES AND OBSERVATIONS

[36]

"Sharpen the sword and fight the battle in a heroic way.

Important note—One doesn't know what information will be of use in the future."

---

[36]

By this time, you have read about all the factors essential for fundamental analysis. Apart from that, following certain actions and feeding them into the subconscious mind helps set foot in the market in a more convenient and probable manner. Let's discuss the same one by one.

I. Requirements of an investor:

a. Demat account:

For investment purposes, the Demat service provider charging the lowest amount as broker charges, annual maintenance and other charges should be one's priority. There are multiple brokerage houses providing Demat accounts with nominal AMC charges per annum and zero brokerage charges in case of delivery transaction i.e. purchasing securities for cash and holding it in Demat account for more than a day. An investor's target would not be to often purchase and sell securities. Hence, he should prefer a broker who provides the lowest or zero brokerage facility in the delivery transactions of securities. In case you hold one with greater charges, just try to switch to a new one. You can do so even along with transferring your existing holdings from the existing Demat account to a new Demat account.

b. Tools of analysis of information gathered:

Needless to mention, managing all the data of analysis in a proper MS Excel file and observations in MS Word or Notepad will be quite useful. So use only that method to store all the data. I am adding this section to warn people who may develop a habit of only watching data over various platforms and analyzing the data and ratios with the help of a calculator or diary before taking an investment decision. It is preferred to have all the data stored in Excel and Word files to perform various analyses at the same time and also for proper storage for future references. It will be of great help in the future to sell or hold your investments.

c. Screeners and the sort of analysis:

As discussed earlier, we need to do the preliminary screening of stocks with the help of a screener as it is not feasible to analyze the factors of screening one by one for the 5000 plus stocks available in the stock market. For this purpose, you need to select a screener which can do the same for you. Generally, screening activity is allowed on various websites for free if you just wish to screen all the factors required, but if you wish to download the same as Excel file for further use, you need to pay for them. I hold the subscription of two screener providers. But if you do not wish to take the screening subscription annually, you can opt for one providing monthly subscription with lesser charges.

Zerodha provides a screener named Ticker Tape where you can take the membership anytime for a month or on an annual basis. So one can opt for membership when required at a lesser charge.

Another one is screener.in, which is very good and provides only an annual subscription.

If you still do not want to spend this much money, then the task is possible but what you need to adopt is as follows:

o   Firstly, screen all the stocks with the preliminary factors to get the results o You need to note down or copy the results manually somewhere else

However, for the sake of convenience, it is preferable to export the screener's data and get the analysis done with ease.

Note:

1. Buying a subscription for screeners is not compulsory but is surely convenient. You can try to get the information by exercising free trial options, if available in any screeners like Ticker Tape

2. I have no linkage with the screener providers mentioned above. I have mentioned the names because I personally use their subscription and these are available at an economic cost. For the sake of readers, I thought I must share the options with them

3. I use two to three screeners to confirm the results I obtain. There is a benefit in doing so. In case certain stocks as suggested by different screeners are not common, you can include all of them for further valuation analysis

II. Requirement of reading annual report:

ROE and other preliminary factors will indicate the presence of economic moat in the business of a company. **After selecting a stock which has passed all the stages of checking, reading of annual report can further confirm the presence of economic moat.** It is important to read the annual report of the last completed year before taking an investment decision in a particular company's stock in order to grasp the idea of the main factors of the business and important management data. You don't need to read all the annual reports except for the stocks you have finalized after the multi-bagger analysis. Furthermore, after getting one stock in your portfolio, you need to refer:

- Every quarter's result and press release
- Every news and announcement of the company
- Every annual report of the company

Till the time the stock lies in your portfolio.

We discussed what information is to be extracted from quarterly results, press releases, news and announcements made by a company. Here in this section, we are going to discuss how to read the annual report in the way an investor should. By investing in a company, you do not buy a piece of paper, but you become a partial owner of its business. But is it feasible for you to look after each operating activity of the business of the company you invested in and also assess whether all the activities of the company are lined up in order to achieve the company's mission and vision? The answer is No. So there has to be some alternative source from which you can get an idea of how the company is growing to respond to its targets. Ideally, almost all information requires you to assess what can be found in the information released by the company in the form of quarterly results, press releases, annual reports and others. So you understand the level of seriousness with which you need to read this information as you have no alternative way to judge:

- Whether the company is able to achieve its objective of consistent growth in the required manner

- Is it able to create wealth over your investment?

See, the regulatory authorities in India have laid down sufficient requirements for companies to release essential facts and figures for investors and other stakeholders through the above-mentioned documents. But the duty of reading them in a way that best serves our purpose lies upon us.

Talking about the objective of reading annual reports, it is the single most useful tool available for investors to know about:

- Financial health of a company, which means the present status of growth in sales and profit along with adequate financial leverage and other factors

- Opportunities sought by businesses to further expand in new dimensions or geographically expand the operation to new areas of the nation and world

- Any future events, the occurrence of which can be proven as a threat to that particular company's operations and profitability

One thing to be taken care of regarding the annual report is that it is a document which reveals all the important information about a company to shareholders mainly, but its preparation is in the hands of the company. So the management of a company tends to present all the facts in a language that sounds like some marketing tool. They give all the necessary information because they are bound by regulatory authorities to do so, but they generally do it in a way such that they are marketing the company. We need to concentrate only on the facts and figures and link these to the company's success in the achievement of its objectives and ignore the marketing accent. Even a company which is declining year by year will not write simply that they are going to collapse. We need to dig out important factors and get an idea if the company is growing or becoming stagnant. Just analyze each word of the management along with financial statements to draw pictures about the present status, growth prospects and apparent threats to the company.

Another idea behind reading the annual report is to know what external factors favour the company and what proves to be against the company. So you will be able to link any future notifications from the government or RBI or any other news with its possible impact on the company's business. In the beginning, you may find it uninteresting, or you may find yourself unable to connect the annual report contents with your multi-bagger analysis. But believe me, it matters. You just commit to reading them with the required seriousness. Soon, you will be habitual to do so.

I have the tendency to keep a brief knowledge about companies' operations and current developments in which I invest in my fingertips. This helped me identify potential ups and downs in companies which was also made sure later by corresponding impacts in financial results of coming quarters. I always read the annual report of every new stock I wish to get in. I also read each press release, result and any related news. This gives me the **feeling of not just being a shareholder but also a partial owner of a company's business, who actively wants to keep track of each business in which he has partial ownership.**

The important parts of the annual report and what to focus while reading them are as follows:

1. **Message of MD/Chairman**

   This is generally the first part of an annual report. This part of the annual report tries to summarize the important happenings in the company during the financial year. It will highlight the company's accomplishments as well as failures along with reasons behind the success enjoyed and the way in which the failures or challenges were dealt with. It also contains information about current performances, a glimpse of the market in which the company operates and how the company will trend towards growth from now. It also conveys the challenges faced in terms of changing market scenario, scandals, consumer patterns, etc. In other words, the chairman's message will provide a connection with the company's vision and mission with all the existing events and occurrences within the company.

Example: Few extracts of GMM PFaudler Ltd's annual report for FY 2018-19 are presented here for narrating what the chairman tried to convey via his message. GMM PFaudler Limited is in the business of providing engineered equipment and systems for critical applications in the global chemical and pharmaceutical markets. Apart from this, its stock often qualifies the multi-bagger analysis quarter after quarter since the share was listed. The extracts from the chairman's message are as follows:

a. Highlight about extending the scope of business by acquiring new divisions and the strategy behind it. This indicates whether the company is acquiring the business which will really be profitable or if it is a diversion from the main business, which is not a good sign for an investor.

"We are pleased to announce the acquisition of Industrial Mixing Solutions Division from Sudarshan Chemical Industries Ltd. With this acquisition, we will create a business vertical that will have a greater focus on the industrial mixing space and will provide our customers with innovative mixing technologies which will help them improve efficiencies and reduce costs."

b. Continuous focus of the company is on what—increasing dividends, innovations and enhanced customer satisfaction measures.

"I am delighted to report that many of 'Mission 2020' strategic initiatives are finally paying rich dividends and have helped us and will continue to help us grow profitably. I believe that improvement is a never-ending process and we will continue to offer our customers new products, innovative technologies, faster delivery time and prompt after-sales service. I am confident that we can continue our growth journey in the coming year."

c. What constitutes the main activities of the company and what to explore more in the coming years?

"The key industries that we serve, Pharmaceutical (Pharmacy), Agrochemical (Agro) and Speciality Chemical (Specialty) all continued to invest in new manufacturing facilities. Agro and Specialty showed a significant increase in investment and accounted for nearly 59% of our total revenue. Pharmacy showed a slowdown in capital spending due to FDA issues and pricing pressure in the US markets but still accounted for 30% of our total revenue. Looking forward, we believe that investment in these sectors will continue, and we expect both Agro and Specialty to drive growth in the coming year. We have also seen significant traction in new sectors such as Oil & Gas, Petrochemical, Fertilizers and Minerals & Metals, and we expect promising opportunities in the coming months."

d. Signals of continuous commitment to remain the leading name in the industry—description about the increase in capacities and other initiatives for overall strengthening of business.

"This year was noteworthy in terms of major projects launched and completed. We continued to create additional capacity for our Glass-Lined and Heavy Engineering businesses. In our Glass-Lined division, we hit a new high of 200 EUs (equivalent units) manufactured in a single month—this was a first for us and will hopefully become the new benchmark for throughput. In another first, our Heavy Engineering division manufactured the biggest equipment with a length of 41 metres, a diameter of 4.8 metres and a weight of 154 MT column, which puts us in a small and exclusive group of companies that can handle such large sizes. We went live with a new cloud-based ERP solution which will help us improve efficiency, decrease costs and streamline internal systems and processes. We have also recently launched an internal budgeting system which will help us build budgets from a bottom-up approach rather than a top-down approach and will also help us monitor and reduce costs."

2. **Business profile of the company and its journey**

This portion further enhances readers' idea about the business of the company by offering more details. This section describes the depth of the company's business by including:

- what it does to generate revenue—products manufactured or supplied, services provided and other operations

- information about subsidiaries it owns (if any)

- the market in which the company sustains and grows

- future opportunities along with risk factors associated with the business

- major steps or setbacks in the past year are also highlighted such as new products, sales/marketing shifts, new services, seasonal factors, etc.

- geographical classification of units and areas of operations and marketing offices, manpower employed, etc.

The company often adopts a graphical and pictorial presentation along with descriptions to depict any of the above-mentioned details. A gentle and calm reading of this portion will provide an idea and visualization of what the company is doing and how it tends to grow. To limit the length of the book, relevant extracts are not being shown regarding this section. You can refer to the same company's annual report as used above. It has a detailed description in its report with easy to understand pictures and graphs.

3. **Financial Highlights**

Often a company presents in the report figures regarding how it has managed to grow over the past three, five or 10 years. The highlights can be in the form of:

- Comparative tabular format giving figures of past years' revenue, expenses, profits, dividend, EPS, DPS, book value per share, assets, liabilities, net worth

- Comparison of the recent few years growth in revenue, EBITDA, PAT, EPS, Net Worth, ROE, etc. with the help of graphical or spherical presentation

- In banking stocks, the comparison can further include Capital Adequacy Ratio, Return on Assets, Net Interest Margin, NPAs, Provisioning coverage ratio, etc.

You should refer to the annual report of one non-banking company and one banking company to get an idea of how the information in this section is conveyed. For example, in a non-banking company, the same annual report of GMM PFaudler Ltd as mentioned above can be referred and in the case of a banking company, the annual report of HDFC Bank Ltd or Bajaj Finance Ltd for the same year can be taken for reference.

4. **Management Discussion and Analysis**

This will be a more detailed version of the business of a company and is often supported with graphs and pictures. This section generally focuses on:

➤ Brief about Global and Indian economy in relation to the company's business

➤ Developments in the industry along with sections in which the company operates

➤ Company's overview and outlook

➤ Financial performance—growth related to last year in various terms

➤ Information on various segments in which the company operates

➤ Opportunities and threats along with risks and concerns of business

➤ Internal control systems and their adequacy

➤ Human resources and industrial relations

➤ Other company or industry-specific information

The annual report of a company provides a part of the management discussion and analysis, information on the above points, by whatever name. The same annual report as mentioned earlier can be taken as an example to read this section.

5. **Financial Statements**

You already got an idea while reading the analysis processes to find multi-bagger stocks how important it is to consider information under this section. The section will include standalone and consolidated financials of the company and related notes. Also, it includes auditor's report explaining the adequacy and fairness of information presented in the financial statements. Consolidated financial statements are to be considered for all the analysis we conduct.

III. Whole process to select a stock finally:

So what you need to do to select a stock which has the potential to provide multi-bagger returns is as follows:

1. Check whether the business of a company satisfies all the factors of preliminary screening as applicable to the type of stock i.e. banking and non-banking. This step will ensure the presence of economic moat

2. Perform valuation analysis applicable to the stock with respect to the category i.e. banking and non-banking. This will ensure whether or not there are hidden negative indications in the company. Furthermore, it will also come to the point whether the current market price of the share is fair

3. Read out all the relevant portions of the company's annual report for the last completed year

4. Read out the last results announced by the company

5. Read out the last press release along with the results announced by the company

Steps 3, 4 and 5 provide further existence of economic moat.

Stocks which provide satisfaction by undergoing the whole of the above-mentioned process will be your final candidate.

IV. Return on Equity— the noblest evidence of the presence of economic moat

Why has the word 'noble' been used here? This is because often revenue and profit figures reported by the company may be in a manipulated form. If any company decides to manipulate profit figures or revenue figures to make the company look progressive and on the fine track of growth, what do they need to do to make that happen? They need to either deliberately report more income or lesser expenses than normal. A company will be able to show more profit in profit and loss account than actual profits. But one more thing to focus upon is what that excess profit will contribute towards the net worth of the company. The net worth of the company will surely increase because profits of the company ultimately merge with the net worth at the beginning of the year and this results in the net worth at the year-end. And if the net worth of the company rises in such a fashion, then the Return on Equity next year will go down. This is because when the ROE of next year is calculated, even if the net profits of next year are not manipulated, the net worth of the company at the beginning of that year would be higher than the actual figure. In this way, the ROE of the second year will automatically come down. Hence, companies which opt to manipulate reported profit figures continuously on a year-to-year basis will not be able to have a higher ROE year after year.

On the other hand, when a company is able to maintain higher ROE of more than 15% in the last five years, this means that the company's financial statements are prima facie i.e. free from severe manipulation and the company is really growing in a good fashion.

V. Consider the book in total and not in parts for learning and analysis in real life.

Some of you may find it feasible to avoid some portion of analysis techniques mentioned in the book. Example: Some may find that checking Current Valuation Coefficient© may not be necessary if they have applied all other criteria along with PEG Ratio. Others may think that financial information is the most important part and therefore reading the annual report is of no use. Some may even apply their brain to find out that tracking news is not at all necessary and focusing on quarterly results is enough. Some may even decide on their own that one or two preliminary screening factors like Debt to Equity ratio is not at all necessary.

I mentioned two things at the beginning of the book:

- There is nothing in this book which is not important to consider while doing multi-bagger analysis

- Learning how to profitably invest in the stock market is not rocket science, but it definitely requires some conscience

Reading the annual report is as important as other parts of the analysis because this is the source where you can find out the exact nature of business along with apparent opportunities and threats associated with the business of the company in the near future. If you have applied time to perform preliminary screening and valuation analysis, then devote some time to effectively read annual reports of all your final candidates. This may provide you with some extra facts on the basis of which you will be able to take a decision in a more convenient and profitable manner. In fact, reading this will give you an indication of what information or news coming in the future can impact the smooth operations of the company and may facilitate you to timely exit the company. Also, the same thing holds true for reading press releases and quarterly results too.

Similarly, involving all the parameters in taking an investment decision in every stage is necessary. Example: The company may have a good profit history, but if the borrowings of the company are beyond the permissible limit and it is increasing year on year, then a threat is there that the picture of financial statements in the coming years may deteriorate.

Also, evaluating the Current Valuation Coefficient© and involving it in decision-making may enable you to find out investment opportunities in quality stocks at a far cheaper rate. Though value stocks are invested with a long-term approach, wouldn't it be better if you invest at lower valuations consistently to create wealth in a quicker manner?

Hence, it is important to consider all the factors and give importance to all of them in an appropriate manner.

VI. Market Corrections – How do you handle it?

1. Small Market Corrections

In the case of small market corrections, there is no need to panic if:

- You have chosen quality stocks after analyzing all the factors necessary for evidencing future growth of the underlying businesses of those stocks

- You keep track of all the recently announced results, press releases, announcements and other news related to the company and keep yourself aware of any possible impact on its business in the near future

With my experience, I have often observed that good quality stocks, which are properly analyzed, provide the desired returns even when the market is stagnant or in a temporary downtrend. There are numerous examples of this concept in my career, but I am providing one of the recent ones. On any online platform like moneycontrol.com, etc, if you refer to the Nifty Index chart for the period ranging from August 2018 to August 2019, you will find that the market moved in a negative direction by around 6%. This means the index suggests negative returns of 6% over the period of one year, but during that time, all quality stocks lying in my portfolio namely HDFC Bank, Alkyl Amines, GMM PFaudler, Atul Ltd, Vinati Organics, Aarti Industries and Team lease services provided positive returns.

And even if there is an impact on your stock due to market sentiments during the small market correction(s), then you can comfortably hold your holdings in the way you were doing before such a correction. After remaining up to date with all the information about the company as released in reports and results, as discussed so far, if you are sure that there is no fundamental drawback in companies, then the stock price is bound to go upward in the long run. Do not be affected by the temporary movements of the market.

2. **Major Market Corrections**

Other than what is discussed in the above paragraph, the market also faces some major corrections. Some examples are the 2008 crisis and COVID-2019 recently. These corrections result in a decline in the market indices by 30-50% and may even be more. Generally, these situations come as a result of pressure on the global economy and often results in the fall of almost all indices representing the stock markets of various countries throughout the world. The reasons can be different each time such major crises occur. The news about the prediction of such crisis comes from everywhere before its occurrence. So by keeping track and reading relevant news and articles, which are from trustworthy sources, investors are able to foresee any such occurrence. In that situation, the prudent practice is to sell the whole of your existing portfolio and wait for the situation to get over the crisis. In this way, you can not only avoid the loss but also keep yourself ready with sufficient cash in hand to take the benefit of opportunity when markets begin to rise again after the crisis. An investor may need to keep the cash obtained from liquidating his portfolio for a few months after that to wait for markets to start rising again. In this manner, they can make better results out of such situations. Another tactic in this situation may be to sell half or a major portion and wait for a turnaround after all things get on track.

VII. Stock Analysis post-COVID-19

Suddenly when the plan of launching this book was about to be executed, market disruption came in the form of COVID-19 which has impacted in quite a crucial manner not only domestic but also global markets. In the wake of this situation, it is imperative on my part to include this section for the sake of readers' benefit.

Since March 2020, almost all parts of India were in lockdown to some level. All production and trading activities except those related to essential items were temporarily shut down as it was the only measure to save the citizens of the country from this epidemic. Further announcement of an economic package by the government and other relief measures along with the shutdown of railways, roadways and airways in normal transportation defined the seriousness of the situation. This indicates clearly that the situation is not normal at all. Since the situation is not normal, can anyone analyze and find value stocks in the same manner as possible in a normal scenario? No.

Since the activities of companies will remain shut substantially for at least the first quarter of the year, the criteria to judge growth potential in stocks will be different from that applicable when normal business activity was possible in companies. There may be a possibility that some companies will face the effect of the lockdown in the near long run and they won't be able to resume the same growth track instantly while some other companies may expect to get promising business activities again just after the first or second quarter of the FY 2020-21. This depends upon the nature of the industry and the manner in which the company operates. By reading annual reports and press releases of the company in the past, investors may have a fair idea of the nature of the company's business and the environment in which the company operates and its fundamentals. But the scenario is quite different and will not easily permit the linkage of a company's near future with past performances.

There may be many articles and news roaming around which attempt to provide a forecast on which industries or companies will be able to resume in a good fashion post-COVID-19 scenario. But as we discussed, it will never be feasible to trust any such report or free material. You need to perform an analysis by yourself. The aspects of the analysis will be undertaken as follows:

Preliminary Screening

You need to perform analysis for stocks in the same manner but only for the period till the end of FY 2019-20. In other words, all the stocks passing the preliminary screening stage on the basis of their performance in FY 2019-20 will be taken for further consideration.

This is because there is no use measuring the performance of companies in terms of revenue, profit, ROE, etc. in the first and second quarter of FY 2020-21 due to the lockdown. If a company has performed well up to pre-COVID-19 period, then it is proof of great underlying business.

The only thing to be kept in mind is that though the lockdown period began from the last week of March 2020, the markets started falling from mid-February 2020. This is quite evident if you visit online and refer to the Nifty 50 price chart. Due to this fact, the last criteria of preliminary screening i.e. change in share price over the last one year and over the last three years has to be seen till January 2020 only. This is meant to say that you need to see how the share price has changed over the one year and three-year period ending in January 2020. If the condition is satisfied along with other parameters, then it is satisfactory to consider such stock for further analysis i.e. valuation stage. It may be a case for companies engaged in the provision of essential goods or services operations that their revenues or profits are not hit in a substantial manner. In this case, one may consider the growth in fundamental factors in a normal manner as mentioned in other parts of the book so far.

Valuation

The valuation analysis will be performed in the same manner with the following changes:

- CFO/PAT ratio and ROE analysis in detail will be conducted in the same fashion for the period up to 2019-20

- The Growth Ratio to be used for computing PEG Ratio will be calculated by taking the scenario up to 2019-20 only

- Current Valuation Coefficient© will work in the same fashion taking into account the PE Ratio at present and Median PE Ratio of the last five years

In COVID-19 era, the factor which will be more reliable along with the above-mentioned procedures will be **Changes in Shareholding Pattern**. Why?

As said above, the analysis of all the factors up to 2019-20 will tell whether the business of a company is strong or not. But establishing linkage between past performance and future scenario will be quite difficult as there will be some sort of uncertainty with respect to each company or industry. As a retail investor, you won't be able to have a broad picture in front of you to analyze all the factors which will impact the company and maintain the growth track of profitability in the same manner after COVID-19 lockdown and resting period. Though you have the information via annual reports, results and press releases, promoters i.e. the persons who are practically involved in managing the company as promoters and managers are more likely to be aware of the depth of the company. So you need to rely upon them for forecasting the future of their companies. They will be in the best position to predict the near future direction of the company and the expected movement in share price too. The question is how to follow their prediction? And the answer is what they are doing with their holdings. If the future prospects of the business are good as per their prediction and the share price of the company has dropped or is static due to the effect of COVID-19, then it is a good opportunity for them to increase their share in their own company and they will definitely do the same.

The case of promoter's holding, as shown above, holds true for FIIs and DIIs too. If as per their expert prediction about the company's domain and industry in which it operates, the company tends to gain its momentum back in quite a good manner, FIIs and DIIs will also raise their holdings in the company in June 2020 and September 2020 quarters.

Hence, the criteria for selection of stocks after the first and second quarters of FY 2020-21 will be:

1. Preliminary Screening and Valuation in the manner as mentioned above

2. Rise in combined shareholdings of promoters and institutional investors

You may note one thing that rise in shareholdings of promoters and institutional investors is mentioned in the relevant chapter to be used as a supplementary input element for taking the final purchase decision, but in case of any analysis done after COVID-19, the same is to be taken as a mandatory component. This has to be opted in at least the analysis post-June 2020 and September 2020 and also in December 2020 if the negative impact on the economy still remains due to COVID-19. Market crashes like this often provide an opportunity to grab good stocks at economic prices, but it also demands little cautiousness on the part of investors before taking any decision.

In this manner, the decision taken to purchase a stock will not be vague as the business is strong and even promoters increased their shareholding with good future expectations. So this indicates enough proof of a great future ahead.

Note: In relation to this topic, i.e. analysis post-COVID-19 period, if you have any technical queries, please send an e-mail to me on my website www.stockmanthan. com. I will personally analyze all the queries of readers collectively and solve the same by way of posting related articles or blogs on my website.

VIII. Other important points to remember

- Never invest with borrowed money. It will destroy your mental peace.

  Taking personal loan at an interest rate of 10-11%, investing money borrowed as such in stocks after doing analysis, earning around 25% annual returns over the money invested and drawing the benefit of leverage—these thoughts are quite tempting to resist. But just remember that on the basis of the analysis processes we discussed so far, you are going to invest with a long-term perspective. But the amount you borrow will have a monthly outflow. Your outflow will be fixed but the returns are not certain enough. This is because any well-thought plan one follows in the market, no matter with whatsoever rigorous analysis, is based on improved probability and not a guarantee. Yes, there is a great possibility that your portfolio will be in a handsome profit provided you follow all the principles of fundamental analysis in a strict manner. But that possibility can never be taken as a guarantee. One more reason it cannot be taken as a guarantee is that the hunt for multi-bagger is often successful when holding the shares for a substantially long-term period, but what if you have some immediate need of fund and you need to sell your holdings in between? In these circumstances, you will not be able to maintain the stress because your holdings are funded by borrowings and you need to pay monthly instalments, no matter what. I would only say avoid your investments being funded by borrowed money as it carries a significant amount of risk.

- Keep ready cash for grabbing opportunities.

It's the normal tendency of an investor to invest all their funds in one go. Even if your stock selection involves all the processes of the multi-bagger hunt, it is never advisable to put all your money, intended to be invested, in one go in the stocks you find. You should always keep some money, say Rs 25k, 50k or 1L or any extra as per your profile, as a reserve and this reserve should be utilized to purchase shares only when:

➢ Either the price of the stock in your list comes at a cheaper valuation in the future i.e. at lower PE but with intact fundamentals

➢ The market suffers a minor crash and the crash impacts some fundamentally good stocks in your list

You should invest that reserved money in such situations only as this will ensure you get the benefit by investing when fundamentally strong shares are available at more favourable valuations, thus providing faster earnings

- Not mandatory that only the stocks shortlisted by applying fundamental analysis will rise in the future as others may also rise. You must have a reason to purchase as well as sell the stocks you chose after analysis. Your selection of stock will be on the basis of fundamental strength and your selling will definitely be on the basis of the stock losing any factor of fundamental strength in the future. See, as a retail investor, you need to invest in stocks which have a strong tendency to rise and you are able to analyze them with the data generally available about the company with all the investors i.e. public information. It is not necessary that mutual funds, FII, DII or some big ace investors like Rakesh Jhunjhunwala, Radhakishan Damani, etc. will choose the same stocks as you will find after your analysis as mentioned in this book so far.

This is because you are investing in that stock as per the information in the form of financials, reports and other data generated by the company. You find that the fundamentals of the company indicate a great probability that the stock price will rise in the future. But the big players as mentioned above may have information about the internal environment of the company or some information about industries or the economy as a whole on the basis of which they will select the stocks they trust. But you need not worry because of this situation as you and those big investors will probably earn substantial returns on the overall portfolio because you both have some solid reason to trust that it will happen so in relation to your selected stocks. You play with your candidates (stocks) and let them play with their candidates in their team. Do not lose trust in your stocks and also avoid trusting stocks chosen by them without having any reason at your level to do so. You can't buy a stock blindly because big players in the market are purchasing it. You may take a decision to purchase on the basis of their decision to purchase, but how would you know when you need to sell it?

- Follow fundamental analysis as the personal oath taken by you

Needless to mention after this discussion that howsoever tempting one stock may be, if the same doesn't fit in the fundamental analysis as mentioned here and as adopted by you, do not put your hands into it. This is because **whatever decision to buy or sell you take, it should be on the basis of properly documented reasoning. The reasoning may be in the form of notes or Excel workings saved in your computer.**

[37]

"One should learn not only from others' mistakes but also from others' good deeds. Both are divine.

And I have both in my account—mistakes and certain good deeds."

---

[37]

This is my experience in the stock market.

It all began in late 2010. I was undergoing articleship during my journey of becoming a Chartered Accountant. Along with my studies and training, I simultaneously gathered interest in the stock market after being influenced by the tremendous opportunities to earn superlative returns by investing in stocks. I tried many things while trading in stocks with almost all the stipends I earned from my articleship. I began with the following approaches:

- Investing based on the advice of friends trading in the market for a while

- Trading in stocks on the basis of market experts' research reports

- Trading in popular stocks whenever there is a dip in their prices

In the beginning, I experienced success with a few investments, but in total, everything went in vain and it resulted in a heavy notional loss hitting a substantial portion of my invested amount. For a month, I tried my hands at intraday trading too, but that too finished with minimal losses as I only tried with a small amount. I looked up the portfolios of my friends and colleagues too. Notional loss in the portfolio was quite common. They were with the interpretation that we should sell when it shows gain and hold while it is in loss. I also searched on Google and got to know that the losers' percentage in India was above 90 in the market. After knowing the same, I was of the view that an overall loss in the portfolio is not incidental and casual. It signifies that something is seriously wrong with the investor community in general. Something has to be done quickly to come up and be a part of the winners who are less than 10% of the total investors in the market.

The experience was not positive at all, but at the same time, there was a firm thought in my mind that many people earned huge and consistent returns in the market over a period of time, though the percentage of people who are able to do that is very small when compared to the whole investing community. They must be able to do that with some solid reason. I just needed to find that.

It is an inherent habit in a CA student that after not being able to clear his exams in an attempt, he tries again and attempts his exams with more preparedness and willingness. I applied the same principle with my experience in the world of stock market too. After a negative experience of around 10 months in the investing field, I was not thinking of quitting the field, but I was very much determined to find out, practice and adopt the principles or methods which all winners adopt in the stock market. I was quick enough to analyze the mistakes I made. I started searching about all the essentials to earn consistently in the market and finally came to realize that the only way to survive the wave of stock market without losing money is:

- Finding stocks having all the fundamental necessities to be potential multi-gainers in the future i.e. have multi-bagger potential

- Creating and managing a portfolio consisting of these stocks in appropriate proportions

- Holding them for a reasonably long term which depends on a case-to-case basis without getting affected by short-term fluctuations in the prices of those stocks

I came up with this finding after taking into account:

- The experience of all the persons around me who were engaged in trading stocks at a similar place without any substantial returns over a time period

- Reading about the persons who made it great in the stock world. This gave me insights that they are all investors on a primary basis and not traders. Two of the most prominent and popular people who inspired me were Warren Buffet and Rakesh Jhunjhunwala

Long-term approach and plans are quite important in life as this is what makes the difference between a poor and rich mindset. A poor mindset asks "What will I get now by doing this?" while a rich mindset emphasizes on "What will I get in the future by doing this now?" Thus, the target of people with rich mindset is quite big comparatively and they choose their day-to-day actions wisely and sync all their actions properly with the required faith to achieve their objectives.

After that bitter yet short experience, I decided to invest on the basis of the fundamental strengths of underlying companies rather than on the basis of the market price of stocks. Now to obtain knowledge on how to apply them correctly, I referred to many books and articles, including my CA curriculum modules, to understand and properly apply the fundamental tests.

During the continuous commitment which continued for about the next two years, while applying the knowledge obtained from my research, I did many experiments on my portfolio and back-tested many concepts along with personal experiences of investing upon those principles with small amounts. I finally came up with some ideal processes and schedules which are necessary to follow for a value investor in my experience. And those who succeeded have used these principles only with little modifications as per their requirements, positions or personal beliefs. The impact of this exercise was clearly visible in my portfolio. It started remaining positive overall, which means in profit, on a continuous basis.

This was a period involving an honest confession as to how I had gone through a difficult journey in the market prior to this. Without analysis of such important factors, I was a fool to get into the market in a gambling manner, staking my hard-earned money. If gambling is not ethical as per our values, then investing in the market without self-analysis is nothing less than gambling. It's simply unethical.

At the beginning of such a transformation, I admitted honestly to myself that I don't know the principles of investing in stocks and I desired to learn about them no matter what they demanded from me in terms of effort. I do believe that honest realization by a person that he has no idea at all about a particular subject is the first step to learn and master that subject. All preconceived notions are to be scrapped from the mind to insert new ideas and knowledge; same as how a cup already filled up with water has no space to store milk in it.

During that tenure, I observed a gradual improvement in my portfolio quality while applying those principles in isolation and felt that involvement of all such characteristics will bring to the table a matrix for improved probability in earning money from investing stock and great surety means very high probability.

After developing the required formulae, I spent another seven years in the stock market with a portfolio that provided annualized returns in quite a consistent manner after undergoing whatever the market conditions were. In this journey, many multi-bagger stocks were identified, namely Alkyl Amines Chemicals Ltd, Vinati Organics, Atul Ltd, V Guard Industries Ltd, Caplin Point Laboratories Ltd, GMM PFaudler (recent) and many others. In the banking sector, the multi-baggers identified were Bajaj Finance Ltd, Bajaj FinServ Ltd, Can-Fin Homes Ltd, etc. This was possible by focusing on companies rather than the price of stocks and multi-bagger return was possible only because these shares were held for a sufficiently long term with patience and strict adherence to fundamental principles. Not only did I confine to these methods with gaining of my portfolio but I always shared the information about the stocks I selected with my friends too. They also trusted the same with their investments and got multiple gains over those investments.

At the beginning of this year, I got an idea of publishing a book for all, sharing all my methods and principles so that others could also find and believe that gaining in the stock market is not rocket science. Adhering to effective principles along with developing a winner's attitude and avoiding all the silly and common mistakes is what makes a person a consistent winner in the stock market who creates real wealth.

At the beginning of my experience in the stock market:

- I opted for what 80-90% investors always do i.e. invest blindly in stocks without proper analysis

- I got what those 80-90% get i.e. a portfolio with an accumulated loss

But the difference lies in what I did after that. After a bad experience, losers think that markets are risky and it would be better to say goodbye to it forever. But I concentrated upon only one thing—"Situation has thrown a knife at me. It's up to me to catch it by the blade and get hurt or catch it by its handle and make it my weapon from this moment." I chose the second one and got a portfolio which is ever-growing, no matter what the market conditions remain in the short- run.

After reading this, you better know what you need to do from now. Prepare your mind to convert the amount you spent on buying this book into the most profitable multi-bagger investment of your life. Just a few months of hard work, commitment and dedication to learn the fundamental analysis and concept of portfolio management are what excelling in the stock market demands. But the irony is that a person can put years of experience to become a professional chartered accountant, doctor, pilot, IAS or even to complete school and graduation or post-graduation to get some job in order to earn a limited amount as salary, but the same person wouldn't be ready to invest a few weeks or months to get excellency in the stock market to make his fortune. If he gains this knowledge and uses this to invest in equity in a manner that can provide huge returns to build the optimum value of retirement corpus, that would be a wonder.

Some readers may just read this book after buying it, but what will they do after that? They will let their findings deteriorate over a period of time without applying the knowledge gained in real life. Sad but true. Make sure you don't include yourself among them. Don't just read the book; make this learning a turning point of your life. If one thinks that reading the formulae in the book in a quick manner and applying it to every stock will make him successful, it may prove wrong on several occasions. **You need to read the book carefully at least three times. In addition to that, back-testing of at least 25-30 stocks is to be done in the beginning to fully understand the power of these concepts.**

You should be willing to put some efforts to find multi-bagger stocks and invest in them, in order to avoid the long-lasting pain of holding a portfolio that may result in an overall loss in the future. Be willing to do that without any excuse. Investors, who have successfully developed the attitude and prudence to find out multi-bagger stocks, do nothing most of the time. But when it is time to do something, they do not hesitate to put in the effort.

Go forth and conquer!

CHAPTER 14

READERS' REQUIREMENTS BEYOND THIS BOOK

[38]

"This book is written while assuming myself in place of the readers and students. I have tried to explain things in the most literal manner possible.

But certain limitations exist while teaching and learning through books—the lack of practical demonstration.

This is an attempt to practically demonstrate how the process is actually done."

[38]

A great level of effort has been put in making this book simple in the best possible manner so that readers can read and adopt all the techniques and concepts and apply them step by step. But the book can never be used to demonstrate how to perform each step of the preliminary screening and then valuation analysis one by one in a clear and detailed manner. So there can be two consequences among readers i.e. readers may fall into either of the two categories after reading this book:

➤ First category of people are those who would be able to grasp all the concepts and processes in the perfect manner regarding how to carry out the complete analysis

➤ Second category of people are those who may get the concepts but also feel the need to see live demonstration of how the actual processes are done from start to end in relation to each decision-making to buy or sell stocks. This is because they seek clarity on how to use relevant websites, Excel workbook(s) and tools to carry out the complete analysis and use the results for the final decision-making

I heartily admire the quick adoption of the knowledge intended to be delivered through this book by the first category of readers, and for the second category of readers, I urge to provide a solution from my side in the form of e-learning by way of video(s); a demonstration on how to carry out an analysis for finding stocks which have the potential to turn multi-bagger from beginning to end.

The video(s) will throw light on the following in the most suitable and adaptable manner:

➤ Short, crisp but comprehensive revision of all the concepts mentioned in the book before showing how to actually perform the analytical processes

➢ The complete process of analyzing either at the time of initial investment, adding on dips or while selling the investment

➢ Method of using various tools for carrying out analysis in the Screening and Valuation stages as mentioned in this book

➢ Providing tools and demonstrating how to create a tool on a personal level, which is quite useful for carrying out a detailed analysis in a time-saving yet comprehensive manner

➢ How to manage the information gathered and accumulated to buy, hold and sell stocks

All of the above is intended to provide viewers with an option to learn all the things in the most practical manner and by bearing the economic cost through distant learning.

Note:

I will be more than happy to know if readers are able to perform analysis on their own after reading all the concepts in this book. But in cases where people are not able to do so perfectly just by reading the book, then they must be given an option to learn the principles further in a more adequate manner.

The sole purpose of this step is to help those kinds of readers only. I do not want any of my readers to learn any part of the process incompletely and cost themselves in financial terms. It would be better for them to put a little more effort and learn the whole thing in a practical manner within two weeks.

As of now, the development of video series is in process and it will be live by the end of the year 2020 or quite before if possible. As soon as it is available, all the relevant details will be posted on my website www.stockmanthan. com. In case you wish to use this tutorial and need an update as to when the video series comes live, just send a request e-mail to me immediately after reading this book on my website with the subject 'Reminder request for video series'. We will keep track of the e-mail ids sending requests and will revert to the same e-mail address when the video series is launched.

SECTION - 5

SUM UP OF STOCK MANTHAN PROCESS THROUGH ILLUSTRATIONS

CHAPTER 15

ILLUSTRATIONS

(Extracts of actual analysis done in the past)

Make a note that the analysis done on various occasions in cases mentioned in this chapter is supported with the base for the decision made in sufficient detail. Each illustration involves a different type of situation where a slight difference in approach was used to analyze the same. While reading, just try to correlate the learnings you had in this book with such bases for utmost clarity of concepts. Read this chapter sufficiently to know how you need to practically think while making analyses in real life.

Illustration 1:

Alkyl Amine Chemicals Ltd

Category: Non-Banking

Time of Analysis   : June 2015

Last quarter ended : March 2015

1. Preliminary Screening:

Factors	Value	Qualifying	Result
CAGR, Revenue, 3 Years	18.29%	More than 8%	Pass
CAGR, PBT, 3 Years	40.98%	More than 10%	Pass
ROE & 5Y Average ROE	24.49%	More than 15%	Pass
	21.70%	More than 14%	
ROCE & 5Y Average ROCE	19.39%	More than 15%	Pass
	15.37%	More than 14%	
Promoter's shares pledged	Nil	Below 10%	Pass
Debt to Equity	0.73	Below 1	Pass
Price Change in preceding 1Y & 3Y	120% & 580%	1Y>0 & 3Y>30%	Pass

2. Strength Analysis:

Factors	Value	Qualifying	Result
CFO/Profit Test for 5 Years	1.16 or 116%	>0.8 or 80%	Pass
Financial Leverage or Equity Multiplier	2.62	Below 4 if CFO/ PAT ratio is between 0.8 to 1, Below 5 otherwise	Pass

Factors	Value	Qualifying	Result
Average of Financial Leverage in the last 5 years	2.75	Below 4 if CFO/ PAT ratio is between 0.8 to 1, Below 5 otherwise	Pass

3. Valuation Analysis:

Factors	Value	Qualifying	Result
P/E Ratio	12.60	Not Applicable	
Growth Ratio	36.93% or 0.3693	Not Applicable	
PEG Ratio	12.60/36.93 = 0.34	Below 2	Pass
Change in combined holdings of Promoters and Institutional Investors	Rise by 0.32%	Better if it rises or is the same. Or at least if it doesn't fall by more than 2%	Pass

4. Action(s):

- Purchased on the basis of the above analysis in June 2015, and in fact, the PE was below the Median P/E of 13 over 5 preceding years from that moment

- Added on dips in May 2016 because PE went to 12.8 i.e. lower than the median value of 5 years at that point of time

- Further added on dips in December 2016 because PE went to 13 again i.e. near the median value of 5 years at that point of time

5. Date till held in portfolio and Reason(s)

Not sold till now. Because

- revenue and profit are on continuous growth track year after year

- the Return on Equity and Return on Capital Employed is always maintained substantially above 15%

- no significant or continuous decline in the combined holdings of promoters and institutional investors after the initial purchase

6. Result

Price in June 2015   : Rs 275

Price in June 2016   : Rs 360

Price in December 2016 : Rs 299

Price in March 2020   : Rs 1,620

As observed, the price moved up in a limited way in one year of investment. It also went down from there in the next six months but bounced back due to intact fundamentals and a gradual and small rise in holdings by institutional investors.

Illustration 2:

Alkyl Amine Chemicals Ltd

Category: Non-Banking

Time of Analysis : June 2018

Last quarter ended : March 2018

1. Preliminary Screening:

Factors	Value	Qualifying	Result
CAGR, Revenue, 3 Years	8.96%	More than 8%	Pass
CAGR, PBT, 3 Years	13.20%	More than 10%	Pass
ROE & 5Y Average ROE	21.36% 23.78%	More than 15% More than 14%	Pass
ROCE & 5Y Average ROCE	15.30% 17.90%	More than 15% More than 14%	Pass
Promoter's shares pledged	Nil	Below 10%	Pass
Debt to Equity	0.59	Below 1	Pass
Price Change in preceding 1Y & 3Y	31% & 85%	1 Y>0 & 3Y>30%	Pass

2. Strength Analysis:

Factors	Value	Qualifying	Result
CFO/Profit Test for 5 Years	1.46 or 146%	>0.8 or 80%	Pass
Financial Leverage or Equity Multiplier	2.46	Below 4 if CFO/PAT ratio is between 0.8 to 1, Below 5 otherwise	Pass
Average of Financial Leverage in the last 5 years	2.25	Below 4 if CFO/PAT ratio is between 0.8 to 1, Below 5 otherwise	Pass

3. Valuation Analysis:

Factors	Value	Qualifying	Result
P/E Ratio	21.50	Not Applicable	
Growth Ratio	13.50% or 0.135	Not Applicable	
PEG Ratio	21.50/13.50 = 1.59	Below 2	Pass

Factors	Value	Qualifying	Result
Change in combined holdings of Promoters and Institutional Investors	Fallen by 0.26%	Better if it rises or is the same or at least if it doesn't fall by more than 2%	Pass

4. Action(s):

- The analysis proved positive enough to purchase, but I postponed the purchase of this stock as compared to others because the PE of 21.5 was above the median value of 16.5 at that moment

- So I waited till the PE Ratio reached near the Median PE which happened in October 2018. I added on dips again in October 2018 at a PE of 16.35 against the median value of 16.5

5. Date till held in portfolio and Reason(s)

Not sold till now. Because

- revenue and profit are on continuous growth track year after year

- the Return on Equity and Return on Capital Employed is always maintained substantially above 15%

- no significant or continuous decline in the combined holdings of promoters and institutional investors after the initial purchase

6. Result

Price in June 2018   : Rs 650

Price in October 2018 : Rs 575

Price in March 2020   : Rs 1,620

Price in June 2020   : Rs 2,243

The strategy to wait to purchase at a PE closer to the Median PE worked out as this proved more beneficial to purchase the share at Rs 575 rather than Rs 650.

One point to be noted is that in this situation, with declining PE from June 2018 to October 2018, the price declined from Rs 650 to Rs 575. But many times, a situation arises that the PE Ratio will decline at a future date, but the price may be more than the past comparison date. This is possible due to the possibility of a huge growth in EPS without a corresponding increase in the share price. In that situation, the stock will be cheaper at a lower PE even with a greater price. This is explained in detail in an earlier chapter of the book with examples.

One more example can be found in the case of Alkyl Amine too. In January 2018, the price was Rs 650 but the PE Ratio was at 27.20. In November 2018, the price rose to Rs 785 but the PE Ratio was at 18.95. In this case, the stock is cheaper in November 2018 even at a higher price.

It is quite good to find quality stocks at a lower price and lower PE in a future date, but it is also fair to get it at a higher price but lower PE. Median PE plays an important role in choosing the preferable PE.

If you did not understand this perfectly, do not hesitate and read out the base of purchase decision again.

Illustration 3:

GMM PFaudler

Category: Non-Banking

Time of Analysis   : June 2018

Last quarter ended : March 2018

1. Preliminary Screening:

Factors	Value	Qualifying	Result
CAGR, Revenue, 3 Years	9.66%	More than 8%	Pass
CAGR, PBT, 3 Years	29.11%	More than 10%	Pass
ROE & 5Y Average ROE	18.74% 14.62%	More than 15% More than 14%	Pass
ROCE & 5Y Average ROCE	20.14% 15.05%	More than 15% More than 14%	Pass
Promoter's shares pledged	Nil	Below 10%	Pass
Debt to Equity	Nil	Below 1	Pass
Price Change in preceding 1Y & 3Y	31% & 138%	1 Y>0 & 3 Y>30%	Pass

2. Strength Analysis:

Factors	Value	Qualifying	Result
CFO/Profit Test for 5 Years	1.15 or 115%	>0.8 or 80%	Pass
Financial Leverage or Equity Multiplier	1.63	Below 4 if CFO/PAT ratio is between 0.8 to 1, Below 5 otherwise	Pass
Average of Financial Leverage in the last 5 years	1.61	Below 4 if CFO/PAT ratio is between 0.8 to 1, Below 5 otherwise	Pass

3. Valuation Analysis:

Factors	Value	Qualifying	Result
P/E Ratio	28.28	Not Applicable	
Growth Ratio	31.27%	Not Applicable	
PEG Ratio	28.28/31.27 = 0.90	Below 2	Pass
Change in combined holdings of Promoters and Institutional Investors	Rise by 0.57%	Better if it rises or is the same or at least if it doesn't fall by more than 2%	Pass

4. Action(s):

- Purchased on the basis of the above analysis in June 2018, and the PE was in fact below the Median P/E of 30.5 over 5 preceding years from that moment

- Added on dips in October 2018 because PE went to 34 i.e. approximately near the median value of 5 years at that point of time

- Further added on dips in October 2019. Though PE was at 44 at that point of time against the median value of 33, the PEG Ratio substantially reduced and reached around 1 from an immediate high of 1.5. This indicated that the rise of EPS in various quarters of FY 19-20 was at quite a greater pace than the corresponding quarters of FY 18-19. Also, the PE was higher than the 5-year Median PE but was closer to the 3-year Median PE. Hence, the big jump in price was expected

5. Date till held in portfolio and Reason(s)

Not sold till now. Because

- revenue and profit are on continuous growth track year after year

- the Return on Equity and Return on Capital Employed is always maintained substantially above 15%

- no significant or continuous decline in the combined holdings of promoters and institutional investors after the initial purchase

6. Result

Price in June 2018   : Rs 841

Price in October 2018 : Rs 918

Price in October 2019 : Rs 1,455

Price in March 2020   : Rs 3,020

Price in June 2020   : Rs 4,440

Full track of fundamentals from the initial purchase till the present date along with track of PE in relation to Median PE was the strategy to get the potential add on dips. It worked in quite a great manner in October 2019. **Remember that PEG Ratio going below 1 and PE near or lower than Median PE is a great opportunity. If the current year's revenue and profits are growing at a higher pace, then consider the current PE in relation to the Median PE of the past three years for add on dips and not with that of the past five years.**

Illustration 4:

V Guard Industries Ltd

Category: Non-Banking

Time of Analysis   : June 2014

Last quarter ended : March 2014

1. Preliminary Screening:

Factors	Value	Qualifying	Result
CAGR, Revenue, 3 Years	29.32%	More than 8%	Pass
CAGR, PBT, 3 Years	16.84%	More than 10%	Pass
ROE & 5Y Average ROE	22.02% 22.60%	More than 15% More than 14%	Pass
ROCE & 5Y Average ROCE	20.40% 18.08%	More than 15% More than 14%	Pass
Promoter's shares pledged	Nil	Below 10%	Pass
Debt to Equity	0.34	Below 1	Pass
Price Change in preceding 1Y & 3Y	6% & 175%	1 Y >0 & 3 Y >30%	Pass

2. Strength Analysis:

Factors	Value	Qualifying	Result
CFO/Profit Test for 5 Years	0.91	>0.8 or 80%	Pass
Financial Leverage or Equity Multiplier	2.19	Below 4 if CFO/PAT ratio is between 0.8 to 1, Below 5 otherwise	Pass
Average of Financial Leverage in the last 5 years	2.33	Below 4 if CFO/PAT ratio is between 0.8 to 1, Below 5 otherwise	Pass

3. Valuation Analysis:

Factors	Value	Qualifying	Result
P/E Ratio	19.96	Not Applicable	
Growth Ratio	18.04%	Not Applicable	
PEG Ratio	19.96/18.04 = 1.11	Below 2	Pass
Change in combined holdings of Promoters and Institutional Investors	Rise by 0.03%	Better if it rises or is the same or at least if it doesn't fall by more than 2%	Pass

4. Action(s):

- **Just read this very carefully. This purchase decision was quite prudent. Why did I choose to purchase this on a later date?** I was not able to prioritize this stock among my multi-bagger list because the PE Ratio was 19.96, which was above the Median PE of 16.5 at that moment, and also the PEG Ratio was slightly above 1. Other stocks had comparatively favourable terms than this stock. Hence, I skipped. But the stock came again in the list of multi-bagger stocks after June 2014 results during August 2014. In that quarter, it was observed that the EPS rose above 30% in the June quarter along with a rise in turnover and profit beyond 15%. Apart from this, the combined shareholding of promoters and institutional investors increased by 3.10%. This was sufficient to indicate a good hike in the stock price in the near future. The price increased from Rs 55 in August 2014 to Rs 98 in June 2015.

- **Understand this carefully too.** In 2015-16, till the year-end, the PE Ratio reached 24 from its high of 38 in 2015-16. Before this, the PE Ratio increased continuously to reach a high of 38 before falling. When the PE reached 24, the Median PE for the last five years was 23 and for the last three years, it was 27.

The reason behind such a fall of PE from 38 to 24 was an increase in yearly EPS from 70.72 in 2014-15 to 111.68 in 2015-16, which is around 58% rise but the share price didn't rise at all. Also, during the same time, the combined shareholding of promoters and institutional investors increased by 0.12%.

So it was almost certain that the price will rise to correspond with the rising EPS. So I purchased some add on units on the basis of this analysis. The same thing happened and the price rose dramatically from 95 in June 2015 to 191 in June 2016, in just one year.

5. Date till held in portfolio and Reason(s)

Sold all the holdings throughout FY 17-18 starting from the middle of the year due to no significant rise in EPS during that tenure and some need of finance.

6. Result

Price in August 2014   : Rs 55

Price in June 2015   : Rs 98

Price in June 2016   : Rs 197

Price in November 2017 : Rs 215

I sold all the units by November 2017.

If you need to understand this better, please refer to this illustration one more time and focus on the above two paragraphs.

Playing with PE, Median PE and shareholding data in the correct manner can make you earn at quite a fast rate by enabling purchase at quite a good rate with respect to the scope of further rise in price.

Illustration 5:

Caplin Point Laboratories Ltd

Category: Non-Banking

Time of Analysis   : June 2015

Last quarter ended : March 2015

1. Preliminary Screening:

Factors	Value	Qualifying	Result
CAGR, Revenue, 3 Years	32.92%	More than 8%	Pass

Factors	Value	Qualifying	Result
CAGR, PBT, 3 Years	68.45%	More than 10%	Pass
ROE & 5Y Average ROE	44.04% 32.75%	More than 15% More than 14%	Pass
ROCE & 5Y Average ROCE	60.88% 39.35%	More than 15% More than 14%	Pass
Promoter's shares pledged	Nil	Below 10%	Pass
Debt to Equity	0.02	Below 1	Pass
Price Change in preceding 1Y & 3Y	328% & NA*	1 Y>0 & 3 Y>30%	Pass

* The company was not listed for three years at that point of time, but other factors were very well satisfying so it was not justified to wait for three years after listing to include this stock in the multi-bagger analysis.

2. Strength Analysis:

Factors	Value	Qualifying	Result
CFO/Profit Test for 5 Years	1.75	>0.8 or 80%	Pass
Financial Leverage or Equity Multiplier	2.65	Below 4 if CFO/ PAT ratio is between 0.8 to 1, Below 5 otherwise	Pass

Factors	Value	Qualifying	Result
Average of Financial Leverage in the last 5 years	2.83	Below 4 if CFO/PAT ratio is between 0.8 to 1, Below 5 otherwise	Pass

3. Valuation Analysis:

Factors	Value	Qualifying	Result
P/E Ratio	38.97	Not Applicable	
Growth Ratio	72.40%	Not Applicable	
PEG Ratio	38.97/72.40 = 0.53	Below 2	Pass
Change in combined holdings of Promoters and Institutional Investors	**Rise by 10.62%**	Better if it rises or is the same or at least if it doesn't fall by more than 2%	Pass

4. Action(s):

- Though the PE Ratio was quite high at 38 with comparison to Median PE of 24 at that time, the purchase decision was made on the basis of very favourable PEG Ratio at just 0.53 along with great growth in revenue, PBT and EPS plus very favourable rise by 10.62% in the combined shareholding of promoters and institutional investors.

Hence, when you face the confusion of purchasing at a rising PE Ratio, the parameters which can be relied upon are more favourable PEG Ratio, overall greater growth in business in the present time and substantial positive change in shareholding pattern.

- **Adding on dips in January to March 2016**

Since the initial purchase in June 2015 at Rs 183, the price rose to around 260 till December 2015 and remained there for a while. Post that, the same started declining owing to fall in Sensex and Nifty for one year till January 2016. It was purely due to the reaction of indices because the revenue, profit and EPS of the company were growing in each quarter at a very good pace in comparison to corresponding quarters of the past year. So the fall in the price of the company's share had nothing to do with the fundamentals. The price went to even 186 and the PE Ratio reached 23 against the Median PE of 28 at that point in time. This was a good opportunity, but then I confirmed the PEG Ratio on the basis of financial data for the nine months period ending on 31 December 2015 i.e. the last reported result period. The PEG Ratio came to be 0.26. Now the situation was as follows:

PE Ratio   =   23

Median PE Ratio   =   28

Current Valuation Coefficient© =   0.82

PEG Ratio   =   0.26

Apart from that, the combined shareholding of promoters and institutional investors rose from 71.01% to 72.20% i.e. by 1.19%. The roadmap was clear to add on dips. The strategy paid off and the price rose from 190 in January 2016 to 400 in November 2016 and even 700 in July 2017. **Hence, the combination of Current Valuation Coefficient© i.e. relating PE Ratio to Median PE Ratio along with favourable shareholding changes and also keeping an eye on PEG Ratio can create wonders.**

5. Date till held in portfolio and Reason(s)

The price reached Rs 720 in August 2017, but from then, it started falling and reached Rs 590 in March 2018. There was no issue in fundamentals until then, and it sounded like a temporary correction in the PE Ratio.

But one thing came in observation after the results of March 2018, the analysis of which was possible after 28 May 2018 (the date of result for March 2018 quarter). The CFO/PAT ratio of that particular year i.e. FY 2017-18 dropped to 0.46 and it was continuously dropping as follows:

FY	CFO/PAT
2013-14	2.31
2014-15	1.22
2015-16	0.93
2016-17	0.71
2017-18	0.46

As we take into consideration the CFO/PAT ratio above 0.8 after taking into account five years' data of cash flow from operations and the corresponding year's profit after tax, the 5-year CFO/PAT till FY 2016-17 was 1.13, and in FY 2017-18, that 5-year CFO/PAT fell to 0.81.

Since the individual CFO/PAT ratio was continuously declining as shown in the table above, it could further decline and also the declining cash flow percentage could bring down the five-year average from 0.81 in the next year.

Other than this, all other factors like rise in revenue, rise in PBT, rise in EPS, DE ratio and everything else were quite satisfying. So the problem was with the cash flow and continuous fall in price could be related to this factor. So I exited from the stock on 29 May 2018 at around Rs 525.

Though I was not able to sell the stock at its highest point of Rs 700, I was satisfied to sell at Rs 525 in May 2018 after being able to purchase the same at Rs 183 in June 2015 and at Rs 190 in January 2016. The stock still proved to be multi-bagger. **It's not always possible to sell at the highest price and buy at the lowest price. Just do whatever is right according to your principles. You will gain ultimately, if not possible in a scrip, then in the overall portfolio. This is the required spiritual development spoken about in the book so far.**

6. Result

Price in June 2015   :   Rs 183

Price in January 2016 :   Rs 190

Price in August 2017 :   Rs 720

Price in May 2018   :   Rs 525

Illustration 6:

Bajaj Finance Limited

Category: Banking

Time of Analysis   : June 2015

Last quarter ended : March 2015

1. Preliminary Screening:

Factors	Value	Qualifying	Result
CAGR, Revenue, 3 Years	35.58%	More than 8%	Pass
CAGR, PBT, 3 Years	31.10%	More than 10%	Pass
ROE & 5Y Average ROE	18.71% 18.55%	More than 15% More than 14%	Pass
Promoter's shares pledged	Nil	Below 10%	Pass
Price Change in preceding 1Y & 3Y	129% & 390%*	1 Y>0 & 3 Y>30%	Pass

2. Strength Analysis:

Factors	Value	Qualifying	Result
Financial Leverage or Equity Multiplier	6.83	Below 15	Pass
Average of Financial Leverage in the last 5 years	6.11	Below 15	Pass

3. Valuation Analysis:

Factors	Value	Qualifying	Result
Return on Assets	2.74%	1% or above	Pass
Capital Adequacy ratio	17.97%	Above minimum requirement of RBI (RBI requirement is 15%)	Pass
Gross NPA (GNPA)	1.51%	Lesser than RBI's overall ratio of GNPA by 20% or more (RBI's overall ratio was 4.6%)	Pass
Provisioning Coverage Ratio (PCR)	71%	More than or equal to RBI's overall PCR ratio (RBI's overall ratio was 59.2)	Pass
P/E Ratio	23.80	Not Applicable	

Factors	Value	Qualifying	Result
Growth Ratio	26.44%	Not Applicable	
PEG Ratio	23.80/26.44 = 0.90	Below 2	Pass
Change in combined holdings of Promoters and Institutional Investors	**Fallen by 0.2%**	Better if it rises or is the same or if it at least doesn't fall by more than 2%	Pass

4. Action(s):

- Buying decision was made immediately in June 2015 on the basis of satisfying fundamentals as mentioned above plus the location of PE Ratio near the Median PE Ratio.

- After the initial purchase, the revenue and profits kept rising in the upward direction quarter after quarter by more than 30%.

In FY 2015-16, revenue, PBT and EPS of the company rose by 36%, 41% and 35 % respectively. Corresponding to this awesome growth, the PE Ratio also kept rising and it went to around 34 in May 2016. **Add on dips decision was taken on the basis of PEG Ratio at that time which was only around 1.** Note that the PEG Ratio still stands at around 1 because of the remarkable growth in the company's business.

- The business of the company kept rising and the revenue rose from Rs 7,298 crore in 2015-16 to Rs 17,383 crore in 2018-19. The corresponding effect was visible in the market price too. Add on dips were made on five different occasions from second purchase with respect to favourable Current Valuation Coefficient© and favourable PEG Ratio at each time.

- Around three-fourth of the units were sold from February 2020 to March 2020 because the global markets were tantamount to crash and usually banking sector stocks suffer very badly in such situations due to the economic crisis caused by the COVID-19 pandemic.

5. Result

Price in June 2015 : Rs 475

Price in July 2016 : Rs 865

Price in June 2017 : Rs 1,350

Price in June 2018 : Rs 2,245

Price in June 2019 : Rs 3,620

Price in February 2020 : Rs 4,585

Price in April 2020 : Rs 2,546

As you observe, the market price evolution over a period of four years was so dramatic.

The gain achieved in this type of scenario is possible only when investors keep increasing their holdings with the rising price of stock repeatedly if the company's financial results prove its fundamental strength at every occasion. Furthermore, confirming the decision by checking valuation employing the concepts of PEG Ratio and Current Valuation Coefficient© is the key. I took a decision of adding on dips on various dates till September 2019 and what would have been the final result after these many years can be predicted by referring to the above-mentioned price data.